Table of Contents

PUBLISHER'S PREFACE

As you read Fr. Laurentin's book, you will surely notice the faults and mistakes of the visionaries of Medjugorje. You will find the same among some of the people who are close to them. Human imperfections may lower the esteem observers accord to the seers and their associates, but they do not disprove the authenticity of Our Lady's appearances in Medjugorje — no more than human frailties in key Biblical figures invalidate the genuineness of God's extraordinary favour towards them.

At the beginning of Abram's journey, God spoke to him at Haran, and at Shechem. (Gn 12:1-3, 7) Only a short time after that, afraid for his life, he lied to the Egyptians, declaring his wife to be his sister. (Gn 12:10-20) Did this lie refute the assertion that Abram heard God's directions not long before? Did it cast doubt on the many divine locutions and apparitions he received throughout his life? Did he no longer deserve the accolade: "Abram put his faith in Yahweh, and this was reckoned to him as uprightness"? (Gn 15:6, Rom 4:3, Gal 3:6, Jas 2:23)

We will not go into details here, but let it be said that aberrant behaviour can also be found among other richly graced ancestors of Jesus: Jacob, David, and Solomon, to name only three.

In the Gospel, a famous falsification of truth came from the mouth of St. Peter himself. At the high-priest's courtyard, on the night Jesus was arrested, the servant girl asked if he was with Jesus. Out of fear, he gave this answer, "I do not know the man." (Mt 26:74) Can this denial be used to demonstrate that Peter never saw Moses and Elijah on the hill of the Transfiguration? Should we wonder if he really met Jesus on Easter Sunday? After God speaks to a man, must he then become superhumanly immune to intimidation?

Jesus said, "Stop judging by appearances, but judge justly." (Jn 7:24) Should not the visionaries of Medjugorje be evaluated by the same standards as those used for Abram, Peter, and the others?

Also, can a high priest be in the wrong? Consider the following and decide for yourself. "The high priest put a second question to him saying, 'Are you the Christ, the Son of the Blessed One?' 'I am,' said Jesus, 'and you will see the Son of man seated at the right hand of the Power and coming with the clouds of heaven.' The high priest tore his robes and said, 'What need of witnesses have we now? You heard the blasphemy. What is your finding?' Their verdict was unanimous: he deserved to die." (Mk 14:61-64)

Examine also the account of how the high priest treated Peter and John in Acts 4:1-22.

Jesus cautioned, "You know that, among the Gentiles, rulers lord it over their subjects, and the great make their authority felt. It shall not be so with you..." (Mt 20: 25-26).

It is essential and necessary to evaluate alleged visions carefully and thoroughly. It is crucial to do this in "justice, mercy and good faith" not staining out gnats and swallowing camels," and not to "shut up the kingdom of Heaven in people's faces, neither going in yourselves nor allowing others to go in who want to." (Mt 23:23-24, 13)

It is vital to be able to open one's heart and mind to discern and perceive the possibility of "the way to peace," not to have it "hidden from your eyes," but to "recognise the moment of your visitation." (Lk 19:42-44)

It is important to judge, not according to some hostile and biased agenda, but in compliance with the norms set out by the Magisterium of Holy Mother Church — looking honestly at the total picture including the "fruits" which are prescibed as criteria by Jesus Christ Our Lord .

— Andrew Yeung

INTRODUCTION

Fr. René Laurentin, Marian theologian and authentic defender of Medjugorje in his recent book has made a significant effort to present and review many of the principal people, events and facts in a positive and humble manner.

Rising above the endless controversy that has surrounded Medjugorje is the incontrovertible evidence of more than 12 million pilgrims who have journeyed to Medjugorje. Countless thousands who experienced Mary's love and call to Jesus her son have returned home reconciled and evangelized.

The reading of this book is an enrichment I encourage.

✠ M. Pearse Lacey
Retired Auxiliary Bishop of Toronto

DEDICATION

I respectfully and cordially dedicate this 17th volume of *The Latest News* to Mgr. Peric, bishop of Mostar. At his request, this will the last one. I hope that this act of peace will bring peace to Medjugorje and the Franciscans: that his ecumenical charism will reach that dark yet luminous spot which has been entrusted to his pastoral care.

To all the priests of the Medjugorje parish who peacefully, and against all odds, cultivate the spiritual fruit which Our Lady freely nurtures in Medjugorje.

To all the directors of periodicals and bulletins (listed on page 13) who have contributed to these annual attempts at synthesis and whom I trust will continue to distribute information within their spiritual axis and beyond all controversies.

To all those who have helped me with research, procuring documents and photos which have allowed me to pursue this inquiry.

To the organizers of the many private pilgrimages to this village where the Church bears so much fruit.

ATTENTION

Wherever I mention "Our Lady" or "the visionaries," it is by no means my intention to pass judgement on, nor contest, Msgr. Peric's decision that nothing which the Church has not judged should be taught. When I use these terms, it is simply to avoid perpetual repetition, using direct expressions rather than saying: "the presumed visionaries" or "She in whom the alleged visionaries think they recognize Our Lady." Direct language is not only simpler but also the farthest from all controversy into which would fall prudent precautions. I will state this here once and for all. My role as an expert is simply to present the facts, to dissipate confusion and to enlighten a field shrouded by passionate fog. Thank God, the Church allows for great freedom in these matters, respecting others and Authority.

The visionaries of Medjugorje

As is the custom, they are designated by their given names:

Ivan DRAGICEVIC, born May 25, 1965, married October 23, 1994 to Laureen Murphy from Boston; one daughter: Kristina-Maria, born in Boston October 25, 1995.

Ivanka IVANKOVIC, born June 21, 1966, married December 29, 1986 to Rajko Elez; 3 children: Kristina, Josip and Ivan (born February 11, 1994).

Jakov COLO, born March 6, 1971, married April 11, 1993 to Anna-Lisa Barozzi; one daughter, Ariana-Maria, born in January 1995 in Italy and one son, David, born in September, 1996.

Marija PAVLOVIC, born April 1, 1965, married April 1, 1993 to Paolo Lunetti; three children: Mikaele, born July 14, 1994; Francesco Maria, born January 24, 1996 and Marco Maria born July 19, 1997.

Mirjana DRAGICEVIC, born March 18, 1965, married to Marko Soldo September 16, 1989; 2 children: Marija, born December 8, 1990 and Veronika, born April 19, 1994.

Vicka IVANKOVIC, born September 3, 1964.

All six visionaries were born in Bijakovici. Also born there was Milka Pavlovic, Marija's sister and visionary for one day, June 24, 1981; married July 17, 1994; she recently gave birth to her first daughter.

Also the second generation visionaries:

Jelena VASILJ, born May 14, 1972, second daughter of Grgo and Stefica, continuing her studies in Rome.

Marijana VASILJ (same surname but unrelated), born October 5, 1971, married to Dinko Juricic, enlisted in the Croatian army in early 1994. Very reserved, just like Ivanka.

ABBREVIATIONS

This book contains information gathered directly in Medjugorje as well as from contributions by the various publications and bulletins, which we gratefully acknowledge. We decided to use abbreviations and initials in order to facilitate the reading.

AB   Alberto Bonifacio, Italian bi-monthly bulletin. It contains the monthly message and the chronicle of the major events.

DN   R. Laurentin: *Dernières Nouvelles (Latest News from Medjugorje):* 17 volumes, printed annually to review the preceding year in Medjugorje. It is followed by the number of the publication.

E   Sister Emmanuel of the Beatitudes Community who resides in Medjugorje; also a bi-monthly bulletin sent by fax.

Echo   *The Echo of Medjugorje*, 18, allée Thévenot, F 39100 Dole.

Eco   *Eco di Maria*, 46100 Mantova, Italy.

Et   *L'Etoile*, B.P. 434, 53104 Mayenne Cedex.

EM   *Enfants de Medjugorje (Children of Medjugorje)*: Monthly information bulletin, edited by Sister Emmanuel.

GA   *Gebetsaktion Maria*, Postfach, A 1153, Vienna, Austria.

MG   *Medjugorje Genova.*

MM   *Medjugorje Magnificat*, published by C. Clause, 01480 Frans, France.

NM *Nouvelles de Medjugorje*, monthly bulletin, founded by J. and U. Costermans and continued by Robert and Dorothée Van Holm, 5, avenue Chant-d'Oiseau, B 1150 Brussels, fax: 322.77.17.336.

Ns *Notre-Dame de Medjugorje*, 74700 Sallanches.

O *Oasis*, Newsletter, 25, Route du Cordon, 74700 Sallanches.

P *Press Bulletin Medjugorje*, Information Centre MIR B 266, Medjugorje.

S *Sakramento*, 67, rue L.A.-Blanqui, BP 85, 93141 Bondy Cedex.

St *Stella Maris*, Ch 1631, Hauteville, Switzerland.

T *Medjugorje Torino*, Regina Pacis prayer group periodical, 9, 1993, #51-54 and #10, 1994.

I thank each and everyone who sent me information, documents and photos, especially A. Bonifacio, Sister Emmanuel and P. Iacopini.

Crossroads

Grace and fruit continue in Medjugorje, despite hardships, contradictions and growing discussions, which are apparently inextricable.

I hesitated to prepare this last annual volume — not less for reasons of age (I'm not afraid of work), than because of the opposition on all levels from Christians whom I respect and admire. I dislike going against the flow and to wrestling with continuous arguments. I prefer investing in peace and contemplation when I write on the Holy Trinity.

I am here again this year to alleviate the confusion surrounding Medjugorje. Pilgrims cannot understand how the grace which is the source of their conversion, of their spiritual springboard, or their reunion with God, is slandered and fought on all fronts:

— You are breaking away from the Church, or:

— You are in complete disobedience, they are told, with arguments of authority which are more considerable and impressive.

This 17th volume seems necessary to clarify these confusions. Chapters 3 and 4 will address this matter. Some of these slogans will be analyzed:

— Pilgrimages are forbidden.

— It is even forbidden to believe in it.

— "Medjugorje is power, sex and money," according to a former pilgrim who now seeks to destroy what he once worshipped.

This book will present the reasons for believing according to the Church's traditional criteria, with all respect to the opponents, and Christian liberty, in accordance with the humble status of the apparitions. It will not stop the objections.

The negative current is taking on more and more of an official value. The local bishop, successor of the Apostles who has authority over the diocese of Mostar, is declaring his negative convictions more and more clearly.

That is enough, some would say. It would be much more advantageous and simple for our human peace of mind, but the bishop states precisely that he has not officially decided anything. He is waiting and hoping that Rome will make the decision and release him from it.

I did not believe such a novel approach was possible, considering past history. Rome always avoided compromising itself in such minor and conjectural matters. Today, we can see the first hints of such a reversal in a document on the apparitions from Cardinal Seper (1978). The *Congregation for the Doctrine of Faith* is taking charge of this matter. It is not content with handing down directives to the Bishops either encouraging or discouraging them, either recognizing or condemning. It is taking full charge of the investigation without visiting the site, as is usual in such cases, judging in secrecy and without any implication on the part of the local bishop, for fear that he might become judge and jury. This would either play against the recognition of Civitavecchia as hoped for by Bishop Grillo, or against the rejection of Medjugorje if the *Congregation for the Doctrine of Faith* takes charge of it as it did for Civitavecchia.

This is adding a new unknown to any prognosis one might make.

One may argue, in order to justify one's conviction:

— The Pope is in favor of Medjugorje. He has officially asked on many occasions to make a pilgrimage to Medjugorje (which has not yet been granted).

— "It is his private opinion," we are told.

— Exactly, as is that of the bishop whose freedom he also respects.

This division is distressing to those for whom things seem so simple in the sight of Our Lord and Our Lady.

This situation is more normal than it seems for the Church, a place of unity and obedience but also a place of liberty and initiative. Initiatives are often persecuted without being burnt at the stake, as in the case of Joan of Arc whose charisms were embarrassing. Dom Bosco ended in desolation. The Pope turned against him and refused to listen to him. Padre Pio was persecuted during his whole life, blamed by a decision from the *Holy See*, which dated back to World War I. That persecution only ended with his death.

— Chapter 1 —
THE SIXTEENTH
ANNIVERSARY: JUNE 25, 1997

June 24, anniversary of the first contact

The sixteenth anniversary of Medjugorje began on June 24, in remembrance of that memorable day when Our Lady appeared to Mirjana and Ivanka from up on the hill. That day is remembered with a *march for peace*, a tradition that began during the war in 1992.

— "But the war is over," one might say.

Yes, the armed conflict is over but not the ethnic conflict, nor are the administrative and media conflicts against Medjugorje: they are more severe than ever, as are the unresolved tensions in the church between the Franciscans and the secular priests. Amidst these long-lasting conflicts, we must stand firm in our hope and our prayers.

This sixth march was the most numerous to date: 7,000 participants along with the visionaries and the Blessed Sacrament, from the Franciscan monastery in Humac to St. James in Medjugorje, singing and praying fervently in good order.

The procession left at 7 a.m. after a 15 minute prayer service. It would end thirteen kilometers later with final supplications at the parish church. "An immense crowd and an immense peace," summarized Sister Emmanuel.

The event was necessary as terrible conflicts were exploding all around.

The five continents were represented. That night Ivan invited the pilgrims to the nocturnal apparition of Our Lady on the hill. She came accompanied by three angels. ("That is a very rare event," noted Sister Emmanuel in her July 1st bulletin.) Many hearts were overwhelmed and converted that night. Ivan said: "Gospa expressed a very special joy tonight."

Celebrations and apparitions of June 25th

The next day, June 25th was the anniversary of the first apparition on the hill. A record crowd of between thirty and fifty thousand people was present, according to the newspapers, along with 212 priests, including three bishops:

Monsignor Frane Franic, Archbishop Emeritus of Split, Monsignor Pavel Hnilica, a Slovak residing in Rome and a close friend of the Pope, and Monsignor F. Bétancour Tirado, Archbishop of Manizales, Colombia.

Forty thousand communions were distributed on the day of the 16th anniversary. Many pilgrims had arrived barefoot as in Fatima. This relatively new penance is growing in popularity in Medjugorje as a means of expressing one's contrition.

Mass was presided over by Father Gabriel Jurisic and concelebrated with 212 priests representing 31 different countries. Masses in fifteen languages were celebrated in the sanctuary.

Our Lady's annual apparition to Ivanka

Our Lady kept her promise with this twelfth annual visit. It lasted about six minutes. Ivanka related these few words: "Our Lady spoke to me about the fifth secret."

Ivanka also transmitted the following message:

Dear children, pray with your heart in order to know how to forgive and be forgiven. I thank you for your prayers and for the love you give me.

A manifesto

Confronted by mounting opposition and negative rumors against what pilgrims believe to be messages from Our Lady, the *Committee for the Queen of Peace* wrote a manifesto, which was not published until July 25, 1997 in *Slobodna Dalmacja*.

It is both a thanksgiving and a warning, against the unjust and increasing attacks this place of grace must face. Those who signed the manifesto insist on the five major points of the message: The Eucharist, the Word of God, monthly confession, the rosary and fasting.

Lukas Pavlovic, Vicar General of Mostar, published the bishop's critical point of view in that same newspaper on September 12, 1997.

This document emanates from a group of Charismatics, characterized by their lack of obedience to the Church's legal authorities who are responsible for judgement and legality in these matters. [...] The letter is signed by the committee's seven secretaries [...] and takes a stand for what we call the apparitions, disregarding the diocesan bishop's stand on the matter and taking it directly to the Pope. They had no qualms about using the Pope's name, or his authority. The mass media and the Church did not pay attention to their letter. The committee must be reminded of the responsibility they have toward the diocese where these events are taking place, and a filial devotion for the truth as pertains to Our Lady (Mostar, August 5th 1997).

Beyond the fervent serenity of the anniversary, nothing has been settled. The bishop remains vigilant and negative. Trust in Our Lady is expressed with fervor during daily Mass.

— Chapter 2 —
NEWS OF THE VISIONARIES

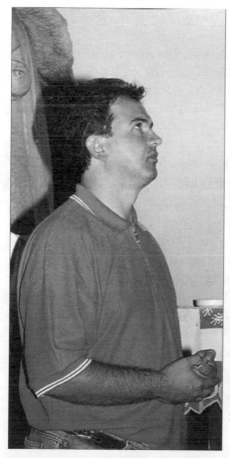

Ivan

On the 4th of July, Ivan celebrated on Podbrdo (discreetly and privately) the 15th anniversary of the prayer group he founded. The group has persevered in spite of Ivan's long absences (*Eco*, 135, p. 6). The group meets in all seasons and in all weathers, Tuesdays on Podbrdo and Fridays on Krizevac (hill of the Cross). Ivan states that Our Lady personally chose each member of the group. They have enrolled in her school for four years in order to prepare for their future mission: marriage or celibacy.

Ivan remains a discreet and wise man, profoundly convinced of the role of the *family* and of education. This is a favorite theme of his when pilgrims come to visit.

Education begins in the family at a very young age. One does not easily change one's habits at 20 or 25 years of age. Therein lies the importance of parents who have love and authority for their children and pray as a family.

Prayer groups must begin with the family. The greatest fruit gathered after sixteen years of apparitions has been the healing of hearts, when pilgrims renew their lives and rediscover the Gospel which alters their behavior in their families and in society. They thus rediscover the joy of living in peace.

For families, betrothal with the heart is as crucial as is the novitiate for the religious. It allows the couple to bring their faults to light and to correct them before contemplating marriage. Grace is there to help them achieve this (Et, 51, 4).

Ivan is emphatic on the importance of prayer, the fountain of his peace and his life.

In 1984, before going to mass, he confided, Our Lady asked me to tell the priests that she would like us to pray every day for three hours. Through prayer, we help Gospa to realize her projects. Men have turned to materialism and have given God second place in their lives. Prayer, especially the rosary, is a sanctifying remedy for the world today (Et, 52, 3).

He maintains that Our Lady has never spoken of "three days of darkness" about which everyone is speaking, even in Medjugorje (*Et*, 25 June, p. 2).

Ivanka

Nothing is new for Ivanka except for the apparition described in the previous chapter. She lives a discreet, hidden family life; her home is open to pilgrims who are not discouraged by the distance from the church: 2 kilometers.

Jakov

Jakov works in the parish office where Mass intentions are received. He traveled to the U.S.A. at the end of November 1997. [Editor's note: since the publication of the French edition of *Latest News*, Jakov received his last daily apparition; see writeup in the appendix, p. 215.]

Marija

Marija traveled to Scotland for a youth retreat on May 22-25, 1997. Her third child, Marco Maria, was born after months of difficulties which prevented her from being in Medjugorje for the anniversary (*Eco*, 136). She summarized the message of Medjugorje in five major themes for a group of French pilgrims:

1. Pray for the peace which comes from God, first in your heart, then in your family, your workplace, your parish and finally in the world.

2. Pray every day. Pray with the heart. Pray with the Bible, which must have a place of honor in your home. Our Lady's favorite prayer is the rosary, which is a meditation on the mysteries of Jesus' life, according to Scripture.

3. Our Lady asks us to fast on bread and water on Wednesday and Friday. There are other means of fasting: television, tobacco, alcohol, and service to the sick.

4. Go to confession monthly. Find a spiritual director if at all possible.

5. The Mass must become the center of your life.

Marija with family in Monza, Italy.

Mirjana

Mirjana, whose life and witnessing grow more and more profound, was invited to speak to a youth group at Our Lady's request:

> On the 2nd of each month, I pray with Gospa for unbelievers [...] We cannot save them without our prayers and our example. She asks us to give these prayers our priority [...], and to witness especially with our lives so that through us, unbelievers might see God and God's love.
>
> If only once you could see the tears on Our Lady's face for unbelievers, you would certainly dedicate all your devotion and love to their conversion. This is a time of decision and responsibility.
>
> Each of us (the six visionaries) has a particular mission:
>
> Mine is for those who do not yet know the love of God,
>
> Vicka and Jakov pray for the sick,
>
> Ivan prays for youth and priests,
>
> Marija prays for the souls of purgatory,
>
> Ivanka prays for families."

(These words were spoken on July 2nd 1997).

Mirjana received her sixteenth annual apparition on March 18th, her 33rd birthday. The apparition took place in Bijakovici, on Sister Elvira's basketball court for rehabilitated drug addicts. I was part of the crowd, which overflowed the court.

Thousands of pilgrims were gathered there at 1 p.m. when Father Slavko led the opening prayers. Mirjana soon arrived, accompanied by her husband Marko, their family and friends. She knelt at the foot of a platform on which a small altar had been built. On it was a

**Crowd scene during Mirjana's annual apparition -
Bijakovici, March 18, 1998.**

large crucifix, a statue of Our Lady, and some flowers. A
group of young people from the community accompanied the pilgrims with zithers in song and prayer.
Mirjana and Marko recited the decades of the rosary.
Around 1:50 p.m. Mirjana entered into ecstasy, joyful at
first, then serious and sad. At times she pursed her lips as
if to better concentrate. There were moments of serenity,
and then the sadness that follows separation. The apparition lasted between four and five minutes. Mirjana left,
and the crowd dispersed. That night after Mass, Father
Slavko gave the following information:

> *Gospa blessed all those who were present.
> She also spoke of the secrets. Mirjana
> received the following message:*
>
> *Dear children, I ask you with My Son to
> become my light, to enlighten all those who
> still live in darkness and to fill their hearts
> with peace. Thank you for having responded
> to my call.*

A group of American friends who were boarding at Mirjana's invited me to join them for their fast of bread and water, as is the custom on Wednesday. They shared that frugal meal in the basement, which is their hosts' meeting room and dining room. I noted the arrangement and good taste of the furnishings and the pictures on the walls. Mirjana is not only a profound mystic and attentive mother, but also an accomplished woman who puts her mark of quality on everything she touches. That is why she has always deeply impressed the psychologists who have examined her.

Vicka

Vicka with Sr. Elvira.

Vicka, the only visionary who is not married, maintains a total, generous and dynamic availability for everyone. She draws many to Medjugorje. She often visits the former drug-addicts at Sr. Elvira's who are comforted by her communicative presence, her energy and her good humour while she lends a hand in the kitchen.

Vicka flew to Holland at the end of June (*Eco*, 135, 6c), to Italy with Sister Elvira on August 15th 1997, and to the U.S.A. from mid-October to the 25th.

Sister Emmanuel accompanied her to the hospital in Mostar and related the following:

> *Our journey was long, because Vicka makes many visits along the way: the orphans' village, the home for Italian boy-scouts, and*

many families around Medjugorje.

She jokes with the children, prays intensely for a long time for the sick, and relates the latest news from Bijakovici (her village) in order to comfort the families torn apart by that terrible conflict. She exudes such faith, such happiness that one seems to touch a piece of heaven when in her presence. I could not help remembering an article in Famille Chrétienne: *"If detractors saw and heard what I do now for only a few minutes, they would break down and forget their dark agendas."*

[...] When we returned, I asked Vicka:

— "On Sunday you had a fever of 104° F, but I saw you on Monday speaking to pilgrims from your stairway?"

— "Yes! I can't let pilgrims wait. They come from so far to hear the messages. You cannot stay in bed when you know they are outside your door. You don't consider the fever. You get up and say: 'Gospa, help me!' You go to them, you feel like you are going to collapse and grab the railing. They ask you a thousand things, they have their sufferings, their petitions, they kiss you, squeeze your hand. You see only black, blurred, confused, and you say to yourself, 'I must not fall despite the fever.' Gospa helps you then and it passes."
(EM, #40, p.4, NM, December, p. 7).

Everyday she answers questions from dozens and hundreds of pilgrims with simplicity, assurance and good humor. In her improvised words, she is always amiable, trying hard to console and encourage the petitioner. Detractors have a field day, trying to find fault with her; and those who want to take advantage of her patronage try to entrap her as she attempts to avoid their tricks and limit the damages they may cause. Her amiable Croatian temperament and her boundless charity sometimes exceed their limits. Vicka rarely says: "Gospa told me," but people can too quickly use her this way.

OUTCOME

The visionaries have entered the adult phase of a constructive daily life.

— Vicka at Our Lady's service without restraint or limitations.

— The other visionaries at the helm of healthy and holy families, guiding the education of their 11 children. They lead serious Christian and prayerful lives, each in their own way.

They witness as Gospa asks them to, except for Ivanka. Jakov, who had remained distant for a long time, has taken on this mission with conviction. They each have their own style: happy and soothing for Vicka; deep and reflective for Mirjana; full of finesse and spirituality for Marija, sober for Jakov, full of wisdom and teaching for Ivan. All of them are natural, without pretension, or affectation. They owe this in part to their culture and Croatian upbringing.

Many adversaries are scandalized, seeing them travel to witness all over the world. But they are in great demand, and these trips are controlled and usually accompanied by a priest. They only go where the local bishop is in agreement with the visit. They exercise great influence on the ever-increasing number of prayer groups. Because Christians, by their baptism and confirmation, have the responsibility of witnessing, I cannot find serious reason for incriminating the visionaries, especially when I find the good fruit of prayer and conversion which is their only aim.

They deal well with the trials of life, and the risks to which they expose themselves. That is not without merit, because their lives are difficult and full of snares.

At a time when faith is slipping away from so many fervent Christian families, it is remarkable how each one of them is an example in their family and their Christian life.

Second generation of visionaries

What has become of the second wave of visionaries, the two who were awakened to a spiritual life by the climate of fervor in the parish, and who have received the grace of inner-locution: "through the heart"? They tell us to differentiate them from the six visionaries who have exterior and physical apparitions.

Jelena, who completed her Masters degree in Church History in Rome, spent the summer of 1997 with her family. She reanimated the prayer group she had revived last year.

She spent a month *incognito* in Paris studying French, the fourth language that she is quickly mastering after Croatian, Italian and English. Her trip was not revealed until after her return to Rome where she founded a small prayer group and is living in a small student community as she continues her studies (EM, #40, p.6). She is radiant with prayer from the heart. She has a beautiful personality. She has not yet chosen her future life (see p. 189).

As for Marijana Vasilj (unrelated), she continues to live a humble and discreet family life in Citluk.

Jozo Zovko

Father Jozo Zovko, first parish priest at the time of the apparitions in 1981, was blessed with many apparitions before his arrest in August of 1981 and during his stay in prison. His retreats exert a profound influence on those who partake in them. He has the gift of awakening people's spirituality. He is continuing his post-war humanitarian aid, especially in Jakljan (an island on the Adriatic) where a village for widows and orphans was built.

— Chapter 3 —
THE CHURCH'S POSITION

Where is the discernment of those in authority? The situation remains inextricably confused since the jurisdiction, transferred from the local bishop to the Yugoslavian Episcopal Conference, which was dissolved with the dismembering of Yugoslavia, is presently left in a state of uncertainty. The bishop openly expresses his negative view (just as the Pope praises its positive fruit), but is waiting for Rome to determine who will be responsible for the final judgement, hoping that the Holy See will take the matter in hand (see pg. 189).

Let us attempt to throw a little light on the situation after establishing certain basic principles and facts.

Fundamental facts

1. The Church's authority must be respected and obeyed according to all her prerogatives, which are clearly defined by *Canon Law*. Held to account by this Canon Law keep in mind that the Church is, according to the Holy Gospel and to the apostle Paul, a place of freedom: "The Truth will set you free," said Christ (Jn 8, 32). The theme is taken up again and specified by the apostle Paul:

> *My brothers, remember that you have been*
> *called to live in freedom — but not a freedom*

*that gives you free rein to the flesh. (Gal. 5, 13)
cf. 4, 26, 31; I Cor 7, 22; II Cor 3, 17).*

It was for liberty that Christ freed us." (Gal. 5, 1)

A true and great freedom, respectful of others and of authority.

2. In matters of faith, the Magisterium has supreme power, infallible at its summit, in the name of God to Whom it is subject; with marginal freedom of interpretation.

But when the Church judges a miracle, an apparition or other temporal or accidental facts, it does not have the same infallible authority, because it consists of a conjectural discernment. That is why the Church does not commit itself in a formal manner. The Church does not say:

— "You must believe," but,

— "There are good reasons for believing. It is good to believe."

The bishop might even say (as Monsignor Grillo said in Civitavecchia): "I believe, but there still remains the freedom of assessment." Neither Lourdes, Fatima nor any other recognized apparition is a dogma. Anyone who does not believe, is not committing a sin.

The same is to be said for negative judgements, with the following nuance, that if the Church condemns a doctrinal or moral *heresy*, it is justly applying its full Magisterial authority on the issue. As for the rest, its authority prevails for the good order of the Church and that is why, following the bishop's request, I have sacrificed the publishing of the annual *Latest News* volumes. This 17th will be my last.

3. Discernment is an open task, always subject to revision as our inquiry progresses and information is gathered, but also because the visionaries are fallible. They can deviate and are subjected to a barrage of assaults and exceptionally strong temptations from the spirit of darkness.

4. If I dare to appeal in this matter to the discernment to which each Christian is invited (especially according to the *Criteria* published in 1978 by Cardinal Seper on the initiatives of the experts, theologians and scientists, initiatives which, according to this document, are appreciated by the Holy See), I will refrain from passing any judgement, having neither the competence nor the mandate which allows me to do so. It is without assuming any authority which is not mine that I try to evaluate the facts and circumstances in this complex area where the Church itself remains prudent and well aware of its limitations. I have often disappointed pilgrims or interviewers who would ask:

— "Do you or do you not believe in this?"

My nuanced analyses (for Medjugorje as well as for other apparition sites) must not weigh in the balance as *authority*. This must not become a form of verdict. I carefully measure my limitations, my competence and my ignorance for all the apparition sites I investigate: I differentiate between the fundamental authenticity of a *communication* with God in prayer and that of particular messages, especially predictions, which are always problematic. It is more or less easy to evaluate the relative holiness of the visionaries, and the conformity of the message to Christian faith and morals.

Father Landeka, the parish priest, stresses that under these principles, the visionaries "must not be the center of attention," but rather the messages from Our Lady so long as these are focused on the key words in Scripture: prayer, conversion, fasting, the Word of God, etc. His prudence goes as far as not publishing the messages in the parish bulletin. He leaves them

Fr. Landeka

to private diffusion, in accordance with the prudence of the Church. This reserve recommended to experts, does not prevent anyone from personally believing with that confident, enlightened and wholehearted faith that Jesus encourages in the Holy Scriptures.

My work consists in evaluating the positive as well as the negative aspects even if it brings me to a closure, as it is for Medjugorje. The convergence of these aspects is as positive as are those of Lourdes or Fatima (both privileged events) and the objections or negative elements are not any more serious. There has not been an epidemic of visionaries in Medjugorje as there was in Lourdes (R. Laurentin, *Lourdes, authentic documents*, volume 2).

The principles having been determined, their application must be placed in a very particular context, unfortunately passionate, complex and Balkan. The apparitions in Medjugorje take place in a Franciscan parish. Notwithstanding valiant efforts, they were not able to avoid becoming entangled in an inextricable conflict between the Franciscans who for a long time were the only priests in Herzegovina and the secular priests whom Rome would like to increase in numbers as was planned in the document *Romanis Pontificibus*. The outcome has been a conflict without any meaningful dialogue which should exist in all complex matters, secular or Christian. If, on the other hand, tensions and passions prevail, the opposing sides become radical, to the detriment of those men of peace who are in the majority. There follows a chain reaction of revolt and despair on the one side and provocation and sanctions on the other. Divisions and hostilities abound to the detriment of God's work. It is a sad mixture that I do not wish to whip up, running the risk of increasing the bad with the good. The present bishop, Monsignor Ratko Peric who succeeded Monsignor Zanic on the 16th of June 1993 was his aide in Rome in the struggle against Medjugorje. He was promoted as his successor not only because of his qualities and his personality but because of his strength of character, his being more coherent, less impulsive and more versed in Canon Law than was his predecessor. I am sorry that I find myself (fortunately for the last time in these annual publications) of a different opinion on the discernment that I have been promoting, pro and con, despite all threats and disagreements.

Where are we then? Where are the solid arguments, the confusions and the errors that need to be corrected?

1. THE BISHOPS' CONFERENCE OFFICIAL TEXT

Amidst the confusion and the contradiction which divert and divide the faithful, everyone, including the Pope, the *Congregation of the Faith*, the local bishop and the numerous pilgrim bishops, are in agreement on the following points:

— There is good fruit in Medjugorje: confessions and conversions without precedent in the Church, as we will see later in this volume.

— From a canonical, judicial and administrative point of view (which prevails), the official reference document is that of the Yugoslavian Episcopal Conference, to whom Cardinal Ratzinger had transferred the authority to judge on Medjugorje after having refused Monsignor Zanic's negative judgement (1986).

If there is a recognized and official text, how can the positions be so diverse and contradictory? It is because the text is a provisional compromise, extracted with great effort. Cardinal Kuharic, man of prudence and great pastoral sense, depended on the *ex-Yugoslavian Episcopal Conference* to take responsibility for this international, important and fruitful place of pilgrimage.

Cardinal Kuharic, mindful of respecting the local bishop's prerogatives, ostensibly gave him the first place in all the debates and negotiations. At the *Episcopal Conference*, Bishop Zanic always spoke first, attacking Medjugorje with all the flame and conviction he so often demonstrated. Following his talk, by episcopal solidarity no one dared speak unless in full agreement, except for

Cardinal Kuharic

Monsignor Franic, archbishop of Split, armed with his authority in matters of liturgical and doctrinal issues. In October 1988, having reached retirement age, he disappeared from the *Conference,* with the result that the fruitless debates were dragged on for another two years.

Meanwhile, between the 24th of March and the 11th of October 1984, Monsignor Zanic had attempted to disallow the pilgrimages, giving Rome credit for this endeavor. Monsignor Franic would always explain the truth of the matter: "*Official* pilgrimages are not authorized because the apparitions lack episcopal recognition. Authorization is premature. *Private* pilgrimages to this respectable parish, are perfectly acceptable according to Christian freedom."

Cardinal Kuharic, hoping to integrate this international pilgrimage into the life of the Church, helped bring about the solution on the eve of the civil war during the autumn of 1990. Negotiations were arduous, but with diplomacy and with concessions, which are his secret talent, Cardinal Kuharic was finally given the pastoral responsibility he was seeking. He thus hoped to put an end to the confused and contradictory situation. This fruitful and exemplary parish had by then become one of the Catholic Church's greatest pilgrimage sites. The compromise was reached along the following lines:

— This text would not yet recognize the authenticity of the apparitions but would leave the question open, the divided members of the commission having reached no final judgement on the matter;

— The bishops would take charge of the pilgrimages which would thus be recognized on an Episcopal level, such as to some degree the Miraculous Medal, Rue du Bac, St. Bauzille de la Sylve at the south of France, and so many others.

The accord was reached during the summer of 1990 at the *Episcopal Conference of Yugoslavia* in Zadar, but the text was so ambiguous following Monsignor Zanic's multiple amendments, that it was hardly comprehensible. Cardinal Kuharic and the *Conference* decided not to publish it. They would take charge of the pilgrimages officially but without publishing the text.

This taking charge, comparable to the one which was taken by the diocese of Rome for the sanctuary of Tre Fontane, was finalized on October 21, 1990. That day, Monsignor Komarica, President of the *Commission of Inquiry on Medjugorje*, came to celebrate the pilgrims' Mass (and not a private Mass as Medjugorje's adversaries now insinuate). He spoke of Our Lady, but not of the apparitions:

— "I come, not in my name, but in the name of all the bishops of [former] Yugoslavia, including Monsignor Zanic; other bishops will come after me."

Bishop Komarica

They came, including Monsignor Puljic, archbishop of Sarajevo, today a cardinal. He celebrated Mass with Monsignor Zanic (DN 16, p. 24-25) as had been decided by the *Episcopal Conference*. There ensued a great peace and joy for the friends of Medjugorje.

Cardinal Puljic

The situation seemed resolved. That is, until January 1991 when another crisis broke: the ASCA Agency delivered the confidential text. *Catholic Counter-Reform* confirms that Monsignor Zanic sent the text. (This publication was in contact with him and congratulated him on the scoop). The Agency commented on the text, negatively interpreting the ambiguities of the compromised text.

A period of great perplexity followed the peace of 1990. Many pilgrims contacted Monsignor Kuharic, asking him to clarify the situation. Four months later, on the 10th of April, 1991, following a new meeting of the *Yugoslav Episcopal Conference*, the text was finally published with one or two clarifications. This is the text:

> *The Bishops, from the very beginning, have been following the events of Medjugorje through the Bishop of the diocese (Mostar), the Commission of the Bishop (Mostar) and the Commission of the Yugoslav Bishops' Conference on Medjugorje.*
>
> *On the basis of the investigations to date, it cannot be affirmed that one is dealing with supernatural apparitions and revelations.*
>
> *However, the numerous gatherings of great numbers of the faithful from different parts of the world, who are coming to Medjugorje prompted both by motives of belief and various other motives, do require attention and*

pastoral care — in the first place by the Bishop of the diocese, and other Bishops along with him, so that both in Medjugorje and in everything connected with it a healthy devotion to the Blessed Virgin Mary may be promoted in accordance with the teaching of the Church.

For this purpose the Bishops will issue specially suitable liturgical-pastoral directives. Likewise, through their Commissions they will continue to keep up with and investigate the fruit of Medjugorje as a whole.

I do not wish to repeat what I gave in detail last year (DN 16, p. 27-33). Seeing the resurgence of much confusion, let me say that inspite of certain circumlocutions, the text itself is clear on the two points that it affirms.

a. The "supernatural" is neither established nor excluded.

The bishops have not recognized the supernatural character of the phenomena.

On the basis of the investigations TO DATE, it cannot be affirmed that they consist of apparitions or supernatural revelations.

The Commission and the Conference cannot affirm it, but do not exclude it, as Monsignor Peric interprets it today. It is quite clear that the declaration is based on the information gathered TO THIS DAY and so, incomplete. Moreover, the text formally concludes that the Commission, still uncertain, *continues* to work toward a conclusion.

Cardinal Kuharic repeated it until the end of Yugoslavia, and hence, the end of the *Episcopal Conference.* The Conference's position was:

— The supernatural has not been established (yet) and not:

— The non-supernatural character has been established (that is to say — the supernatural is excluded).

What is the significance of the term "supernatural" used by the *Episcopal Conference* in the key phrase:

"It cannot be affirmed that one is dealing with supernatural apparitions or revelations?"

1. The Conference does not deny the evident supernatural fruit of the pilgrimages to Medjugorje. The Commission does not seem to have investigated these remarkable fruits. It does not breathe a word about them, although these fruits constitute a world event.

2. In these judgements, the word supernatural is usually taken to mean "extraordinary" or "miraculous." I have often regretted the fact that many commissions do not bother to investigate the supernatural fruit, but are polarized in an utopian search for a restrictive proof of the unexplainable, otherwise known as a miracle. God does not restrict. The inquiries thus come inevitably to the conclusion: in the absence of such proof, one cannot conclude that the supernatural is involved here.

Nevertheless, in Medjugorje, as we have read in the previous volumes and as we will repeat later on in chapter five, in dealing precisely with this fruit, the beneficiaries have declared 350 healings with great thanksgiving. Among these *declared* healings, which are only part of the whole picture, many come with documents and medical certificates. Two of them have been *medically recognized* with complete dossiers, similar to those we find in Lourdes. Doctor Korljan, president of the *scientific sub-commission* established by the *Yugoslav Episcopal Commission*, explained to me on many occasions why, for lack of time and means, he had selected the two most evident and most documented healings.

— That of Damir Coric seemed to him the most convincing. He had personally examined the original tomographies proving a cerebral reconstitution in that youth on which Vicka had laid hands on the church doorstep in July of 1981.

— In the case of Diana Basile, her personal doctor, professor Gildo Spaziante of Milan, wrote a book in which among others he reveals her case (DN 13, p. 79-96).

The question I have been asking for years and to which I have yet to receive an answer is the following:

Why have these two healings, recognized by the Church's official authority who has since died, been silenced? What has become of them? Why have they been neglected along with the healings studied by Italian doctors, five of which are presented in the best conditions (DN 10, 36-40; 13, 80-90)? What about many others for which remarkable dossiers were ultimately established? Does this conspiracy of silence stem from a lack of interest in the scientific sub-commission? (Doctor Korljan often expressed to me his regret of never having sat on that Commission); or from denial mechanisms often triggered by extraordinary events.

Why do the commission, followed by the bishops, dare speak as if there were no proof, no serious argument for the *supernatural* (as in "miraculous"), as if Gospa had accomplished nothing at all in Medjugorje? We find herein the classic misunderstanding between the healed sick and the powers that be, illustrated in the Gospel, more precisely in the healing of the man born blind in the Gospel of John, chapter 9. At least, Cardinal Kuharic has specified:

> As for the supernatural aspect of the apparitions, we have declared: UNTIL THE PRESENT TIME, we cannot affirm this fact.

We hand that over to a HIGHER AUTHORITY.
The Church is in no hurry. (DN 13, p. 40-41
cf. 16 p. 30).

Meanwhile, Doctor Korljan, an eminent scientist
has since died, and is forgotten along with his works. A
certain magazine attributed to Cardinal Kuharic the
opinion that there "were no supernatural apparitions
in Medjugorje." The magazine and the Cardinal have
denied this negation as we mentioned (DN 16, p. 31,
143-145).

Under the title: "Neither cult nor pilgrimage",
Bishop Peric declares:

> *The bishop forbids anyone from preaching*
> *or from invoking in churches the supernat-*
> *ural origin of the alleged apparitions and*
> *revelations.* (see appendix page 177)

Something that is too often forgotten today is that
priests most certainly must preach the faith in
churches, not particular opinions. That reserve does not
prohibit the faithful, nor the priests, from believing in
the apparitions as did the faithful in Lourdes and at
Fatima, where their faith always preceded and brought
forth official recognition, while respectfully waiting for
the decision of the Church — in the context of
Christian freedom. This also does not prohibit anyone
from speaking about Our Lady in Medjugorje, as did
the bishops who came to celebrate the pilgrims' Mass.
The message can also be preached as long as it is a pure
echo of the Gospel. And God knows how often it has
been criticized for being too repetitive.

b. Taking charge of the pilgrimages

The bishops have clearly taken charge of the pilgrimage site. On June 17, 1991, two months after the
publication of the definitive text of April 10, Archbishop
Puljic, Bishop Zanic and two other bishops convened

and planned for a second meeting on the 27th of June 1991 to take charge of Medjugorje. On June 25th, the declaration of independence by the Slovenians and the Croatians ignited hostilities and the meeting was never held. The disintegration of Yugoslavia put an end to the *Episcopal Conference* of Yugoslavia which had made the decision. The tension which was foreseen between those who wanted to promote or channel the fruits of Medjugorje and those who wanted to stifle the pilgrimages in line with Bishop Zanic's views, disappeared.

As for the pilgrimages, since 1984, the struggle has been constant between

— those who declared pilgrimages prohibited,

— and those who stated each time: No. Private pilgrimages remain open in accordance with Christian freedom, which is not an empty word.

Following the radical or uncertain interpretations of the ambiguous answer by the *Congregation of the Faith* to Msgr. Taverdet, and other bishops (as we have seen in DN 16, p. 33-34), Dr. Navarro-Valls, spokesman for the Holy See and in direct contact with the Pope and his Secretariat, set things straight on two occasions:

1. On June 19, 1996, he stated that no new facts had altered the situation concerning private pilgrimages.

2. On August 21, 1996, he wrote in the *Catholic News Service Agency:*

> *The Vatican has never told Catholics they could not go to Medjugorje. On the contrary, the bishops were told: "Your parishes and dioceses cannot (yet) organize official pilgrimages." Pilgrims cannot be told not to go until the apparitions are proved to be false which has neven been stated; and so anyone can go. [...] A Catholic who goes in good faith to an apparition site is entitled to spiritual assistance. Thus, the Church does not forbid its*

priests from accompanying the trips to Medjugorje in Bosnia-Herzegovina, organized by the laity, just as it does not forbid them from accompanying a group of Catholics who might go to visit the Republic of South Africa...

Reading superficially the letter from Archbishop Bertone, one might think that Catholics are henceforth prohibited from going to Medjugorje. That would be an erroneous interpretation because nothing has changed, nothing new has been said. The problem lies in the organizing of official pilgrimages, which would seem to constitute a canonical recognition of the events in Medjugorje still under study. It is quite another thing to organize a pilgrimage accompanied by a priest, necessary for hearing confessions. It is too bad that the words addressed to Archbishop Bertone have been taken in a restrictive sense. Have the Church and the Vatican said no to Medjugorje? NO! NO!

One cannot be clearer, and the spokesman for the Holy See has never denied or corrected a single word of this text. These texts had to be republished seeing the confusion which remains.

Bishop Ratko Peric himself specifies in the conclusion of his book (see annex page 186):

The bishop has only asked that no OFFICIAL pilgrimage be organized, either on the parish, the diocesan, or Church levels.

He does not feel he has the right to prevent private pilgrimages, regardless of his personal wishes and opinions, which he does not hide. As such, he shows himself to be a very good canonist.

The objections

One must certainly take the bishop's objections into consideration, beginning with the banality of the messages. They have been quite repetitive over the last 16 years: prayer, faith, fasting, penance, etc. What better could be said?

Is it not the role of a mother to repeat indefinitely those things which are essential until the children understand? Isn't it remarkable how those banal messages have captured the attention of the pilgrims and are now practised fruitfully by many of the faithful who receive them regularly?

1. If the bishop does recognize the large number of confessions, conversions, and other good spiritual fruit in Medjugorje, he adds:

> *The fruit so often mentioned is not a proof that it results from apparitions or supernatural revelations [...] it can be understood as a product of the regular work of God's grace.*

Why is God's grace bearing such an inordinate number of conversions and holiness in Medjugorje? Why is the fundamental criterion of discernment given by Christ Himself, "We judge a tree by its fruit," being devalued?

2. "The charitable and humanitarian activities which flourished in Medjugorje throughout the war and beyond, and from which the bishopric of Mostar has also benefited, are not a proof of the authenticity of the apparitions," notes the bishop. Is it negligible that the apparitions have inspired so much generosity, some of which was given at the cost of many lives?

Without doubt, Bishop Peric is entitled to operate a theoretical dissociation between the apparitions and their fruit, but we are entitled to discern their link, which is so evident in the field.

3. The bishop disapproves of having the church of St. James of Medjugorje called a "sanctuary" or place of "Marian cult."

We do not understand the sense of such a restriction, since every church is a sanctuary of the Lord Himself, present in the Eucharist. We cannot see what would exclude the parish church of Medjugorje. That is why Cardinal Kuharic, principal authority for the decisions of the *Yugoslav Episcopal Conference*, had specified that the said conference had taken the following decision:

> *We the bishops, following the Commission's three years of studies, have declared Medjugorje to be a place of prayer and a Marian sanctuary. This means that we are not opposed to private pilgrimages to Medjugorje where the Mother of God may be venerated in conformity with the teachings and the faith of the whole Church.* (*De Vecernij List*, August 1993, DN 13, p. 40-41).

Here again, Bishop Peric contradicts Cardinal Kuharic.

2. BISHOPS IN FAVOR FROM THE WHOLE WORLD.

It is surprising how many bishops come to Medjugorje in spite of the local bishop's opposition and episcopal solidarity.

Why is that? It is because their pastoral calling, mindful of what is spiritual, discerns the benefits of Medjugorje: conversions, better integration into the Church, etc. They recognize this place of grace.

The long list continues to grow in spite of the ever-increasing negative current.

From the 8th to the 15th of May 1997, three bishops visited Medjugorje from Uganda: Frédéric Drandua (54 years), bishop of Arus, Deogratias Byabazair (56 years), bishop of Hoima, and Joseph Oyanga (65 years), bishop from Lira. Before coming, they had consulted with their country's Apostolic Nuncio, Monsignor Luis Robles Diaz, who told them:

— "The Pope does not speak of Medjugorje publicly but he is favorable. Go!"

They concelebrated Mass on May 12, 1997. Monsignor Drandua, a learned man of words, was very successful and received unusual applause when he ended a sermon by referring to one of the visionaries:

Ivan who is so down-to-earth, mentioned that Medjugorje is a school of prayer. It is one of the great graces here. I ask you to find many more students who wish to learn at Our Lady's school when you return home.

(The complete sermon of May 12th, 1997 was published in P, 21st of May 1997, p. 1-2).

During their pilgrimage, the three bishops, men of communication and initiative, courteously visited Bishop Peric. Monsignor Drandua described the meeting:

For him, Medjugorje is not a problem (he told me), because people come here to pray. The problem for him is the Franciscans who, as far as he is concerned, wish to be independent. I told him:

— "Medjugorje constantly speaks of peace. Our Lady invites us to change our own heart and to search for peace in our hearts. You cannot say that the Franciscans are bad. You must accept the fact that you too, must change. Then, the Franciscans will also change and peace will be possible. The message of peace is

manifested in the parish and it has changed you as well as the Franciscans. Have the strength to humble yourself before the Lord and to begin praying for peace.

"I beg you, dear brother, decide for peace! Call the Franciscans! Maybe only a few will come. Everything cannot be accomplished in one day. You must go to them because you are their shepherd. Tell them: 'Come, dear sons, I beg of you, come!' If you do this, I am certain that you will succeed."

He answered: "I will try."

He told me that the Franciscans did not accept either the superior General or Rome.

I told him: "Rome wants peace and you, here, must work towards it concretely." (P, June 4, 1996, p. 2).

He also gave a personal witness:

It has been truly a great experience for me, especially in the matter of prayer. [...] People come and their lives change. Under these conditions, it is impossible to say "that the Virgin does not appear." (P, June 4th 1997, p. 66)

The two other bishops agreed. Bishop Byabazair was impressed by the quality of prayer:

"I was present during the apparitions. I am deeply convinced that they are true encounters."

Joseph Oyanga, bishop of Lira for the last eight years, was struck by seeing so many people fasting. He noted:

"This experience will give me the strength to speak of Our Lady to the people. I feel that until now, I have not given her sufficient attention. She is close to us. That is the principal message of Medjugorje."

During that same month of June, Monsignor Johannes Dyba, 67-year-old bishop of Fulda, came to the shrine while on a tour of the German troops of the U.N.

Adalbert Nzdana, 57-year-old bishop of M'Balmayo, stayed five days in Medjugorje in June of 1997, concelebrating the evening Mass where he solemnly blessed the pilgrims:

> *I wanted to remain incognito, but I found a veritable school of the Gospel here. I give thanks to Mary.*
>
> *Here I feel a fullness of joy. I feel that Medjugorje is the continuation of Fatima. As a matter of fact, someone (the Pope) has stated this before me. Here I see the Gospel lived in accordance with the need of man today. [...]Here we speak of life, while in the world it is death that we experience* (P. 68, p. 2).

Monsignor Damien Kyaruzi, Vicar General of Bukoba (Tanzania), visited Medjugorje on a trip to Rome to receive the episcopal consecration (end of May):

> *I come here to pray and to prepare myself [...] I saw here a great piety [...] Medjugorje is not only a place of prayer, it is a place of great apprenticeship* (P, 68, p. 2).

Monsignor Fabio Betancur Tirado, 59-year-old archbishop of Manizalès in Colombia, came for the 1997 anniversary along with 56 pilgrims of which four were priests:

> *It is the first time that I come here, and I perceive the presence of God here* (P, July 1997, p. 1-2).

Monsignor Stephen Fumio Hamao, 67-year-old bishop of Yokohama, president of the Episcopal Conference of Japan, who came to Medjugorje on the 16th of August, spoke at length with Father Ivan Landeka, the pastor of Medjugorje.

Monsignor Arokiasamy, 70-year-old bishop of Madurai India, came in August 1997. He declared:

Many healings have been attributed to Our Lady's intercession: physical healings and spiritual conversions [...] The fact that Christians continue to come here in greater and greater numbers is a proof that miraculous gifts are granted here. If this were not the case, the flow of pilgrims would have ceased long ago. "You can fool some of the people some of the time, but you cannot fool all of the people all of the time," he concluded with Chesterton.

Aware of the difficult situations, he added:

The Church is taking its time but has not prohibited pilgrimages. What saddens me most is the negative attitude taken by the local bishop along with his predecessor's. Let us pray that this negative position might change (P, 72, p. 2).

In private, the Pope encourages pilgrimages to Medjugorje, and approves of them. That is sufficient for us now.

Monsignor Joâo Evangelist Martins Terra, SJ, 71–year-old auxiliary-bishop of Brasilia, capitol of Brazil, visited Medjugorje in November 1997. During a long interview he declared:

"I have the feeling that the village and its surroundings live only for Gospa."

Monsignor André Fernand Anguilé, 75-year-old bishop of Libreville in Gabon, came just before September 15, 1997. He had been dissuaded from coming before learning from a more reliable source that private pilgrimages are not prohibited. He had planned on staying for three days, but prolonged his visit:

Ivan's fervent prayer and apparition conquered me. I would be happy to see priests from Gabon coming here, if they so wish.

Monsignor Patrick Power, 55-year-old auxiliary bishop from Canberra, Australia, came to Medjugorje in February of 1998. He expressed his deepest impressions thus:

I have been a priest for 33 years and a bishop for 12 years [...] I've had a very unusual experience. In January 1993, I attended a prayer service in Canberra along with Father Slavko and the visionary Ivan. I was profoundly touched by what I had seen and heard. The message given by Ivan and the manner in which it was done moved me deeply. He spoke of peace, love, conversion, penance, fasting and profound faith. These are messages I've often heard and about which I have spoken myself, but the simplicity with which it was said had an exceptional significance for me [...]

In May of 1993, I had taken some free time to come to Medjugorje incognito. The war was still raging [...] Many things impressed me. I was already a bishop, but had come as a private person [...]

This then is the second time I have come to Medjugorje; this time with a group of Australian pilgrims including my sister and her three children [...] Gospa granted me many graces. I found a deep peace here especially after hearing Vicka's witnessing, the same peace I felt in 1993, while listening to the messages the first time. This experience is helping me to renew my vocation as a priest, and my service as bishop. Medjugorje is peace. I've experienced inner peace and shared this with our group. When I see what is happening amongst us: people coming back to the faith, to prayer, to confession, I know I must encourage others to come here [...] I thank the faithful and the priests who work here. Your testimony of faith, love, prayer and hospitality is very important to us pilgrims. (P, 87, March 25, p. 2).

In April, Gerard Dionne, 78-year-old bishop of Edmundston, New Brunswick, Canada, witnessed:

This is my first visit to Medjugorje. The Croatian Franciscans who work in my diocese had spoken to me about it. I have heard for 17 years now, and not only from them, of the Gospa's daily apparition. This fact was somewhat surprising to me and I didn't know if I should believe it.

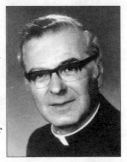

Bishop Dionne

This year a group of pilgrims asked me to be their spiritual guide on this trip. It was a wonderful gift for me, as I wanted to see with my own eyes what is happening here. Everything I saw during this pilgrimage touched me deeply. [...]

The faith of the villagers, the daily attendance at Mass and the spirit of devotion were remarkable. I saw people in large numbers scaling the hills which are not easily climbed, confessing, praying...They came from all corners of the world. That is why it would be difficult for me to conclude that it is all coincidental. It is comparable to Lourdes and Fatima. I cannot give a definitive judgement. That is the local bishop's responsibility. Nevertheless, I can affirm that it is God who is attracting pilgrims here.

I've often talked with people who had been to Medjugorje. Some had come many times, even though the trip is long and costly. Upon their return, they witnessed to their faith with a new zeal. God has awakened their hearts, and through them in the hearts of others, a new hope, through the intercession of His Mother. I believe Our Lady is appearing here. I could not explain it otherwise.

An American newsprint published:

— a list of 128 bishops including 6 cardinals who were pilgrims to Medjugorje,

— a list of 113 bishops including 24 cardinals who have testified to the "good fruit of Medjugorje;" and that list is not exhaustive. (*Medjugorje, What Does the Church Say?* Santa Barbara U.S.A., 3rd edition 1998, p. 14-19 with the imprimatur of Bishop S.W. Treinen).

Other bishops have chosen to come *incognito* and I respect their concern for discretion.

Amongst the many favorable testimonies from bishops who have not visited Medjugorje, that of Monsignor Christoph Shönborn, 63-year-old newly appointed Cardinal of Vienna, stands out. He is one of the two youngest in the latest promotions to cardinal. He was the main coordinator for the new *Catholic Catechism*. On September 14, 1996, this man of outstanding credentials declared to over 10,000 people:

Cardinal Shönborn

"Medjugorje bears immense and marvelous fruit. The Church's position on the apparitions remains open and discreet. The Church has not yet recognized them, but we can give thanks to Our Lady who is giving these signs to our poor humanity."

Coadjutor of Vienna since April 13, 1995, and Archbishop since the following 14th of September, Archbishop Shönborn was struck by the fact that half of the seminarians — young people of exceptional worth — found their vocation in a group of young people that was formed in Austria as a result of the pilgrimage to Medjugorje. On the 26th of October, he authorized Father Jozo Zovko to speak in his presence at his cathedral.

Monsignor Franic's Project

During a ceremony where he was to receive a new distinction on April 19, 1997, Monsignor Franic, Archbishop Emeritus of Split and defender of Medjugorje, gave a talk entitled *"Communism Destroys All That Is Good."*

Archbishop Franic

He confirmed his proposition that the anniversary for the year 2,000 be celebrated in the *Queen of Peace* Sanctuary in Medjugorje.

With the approval of the Holy See and of John–Paul II, he has invited our bishops to organize for 2001, a ceremony of thanksgiving to Our Lady of Medjugorje. It would celebrate all the gifts we have received and especially the gift of freedom which can only be the work of God through the intercession of the Virgin Mary. The Croatian bishops have yet to respond publicly to this proposition.

Archbishop Franic recently presented in Split a photographic monograph of Medjugorje, declaring:

> *The apparitions of Our Lady must be considered as a new intervention of God in the history of humanity. This will only be understood with the passage of time. I have personally heard the voice of Our Lady, although I have never seen her. In the fruit of Medjugorje, that is prayer, fasting and fraternal love, I see the signs of a preparation for meeting with God. Following the declaration of 1991, our bishops confirmed that Medjugorje is a place of pilgrimage and prayer. It has become so for the faithful of the whole world* (Eco 1997, #134).

What does the Pope think?

John-Paul II avoids any public position. He has always respected the position of the two successive bishops (even though Bishop Zanic's negative report was refused in 1986 and the responsibility transferred after consultation with him). The Pope does not hesitate to give his favorable opinion with the required nuances. He recognizes and admits the fruit; he encourages prelates who consult him to go. This is one of the reasons for so many episcopal visits.

Adversaries of Medjugorje have sown doubt on the many accounts of this favorable position, which we transmit faithfully every year from a good source. Archbishop Rodeo told Father Slavko during a meeting of bishops in May 1997:

> *Monsignor Francesco Cuccarese, 67-year-old archbishop of Pescara, asked the Pope how he should treat the people who go to Medjugorje. The Pope answered with the following question:*
>
> *— "What are the people doing there?"*
>
> *The bishop answered:*
>
> *— "They are praying, going to confession, doing penance."*
>
> *— "Then let them go," concluded the Pope.*
>
> *It is also the archbishop's position.*
>
> (P, September 15th).

During a *Eucharistic Congress* in Bologna, Italy (1997), Monsignor Mario Rizzi, 71-year-old ex-

Bulgarian Nuncio, related how in 1996 he found himself in the Pope's private chapel for his daily mass, along with Monsignor Roberto Cavallero of Chiavari, Italy after returning from Medjugorje. John-Paul II asked the latter:

— "Medjugorje, do you believe?"

"Yes, I believe," was the answer. And he dared return the question:

— "And you, Holy Father, do you believe?"

Following a long pause, the Pope declared, articulating each word:

— "*Ci credo, ci credo, ci credo!*" (I believe it, I believe it, I believe it!)

It is admittedly a *personal* conviction in which he does not invoke his authority or his position, out of respect for those whose opinions differ and which he does not share. Those who believe are in no way dissident minorities or rebellious against the Pope, as many accuse nowadays. They discreetly share his intuition of true spirituality.

APPENDIX TO CHAPTER 3

1. MEDICAL TESTS IN ITALY
APRIL 22-23, 1998

In 1984 professor Joyeux vainly tried to run a new series of tests using more perfected equipment, notably electro-encephalograms (e.e.g.) and electro-oculograms (e.o.g.) It would be a first in this field. Today's high-performance equipment does not only register eight fields of data like the portables in 1984, but more than 30, including oculograms, all in one test.

The circumstances were more favorable for the Italian doctors Margnelli and Gagliardi. They invited seven other doctors and two secretaries. Present as support was Fra Ivan Landeka, Medjugorje's parish priest who understood the necessity for submitting the visionaries to a new series of medical tests at a time when an increasing rumor was spreading to the effect that the apparitions in Medjugorje had ceased. The medical tests could help to confirm or to deny those rumors.

The tests were run on the 22nd and 23rd of April, 1998 at Capiago, near Como in Italy, at the Dehonian Fathers' Retreat House. Three visionaries were present, Marija, Ivan and Vicka.

Vicka was there only for some general tests because Our Lady had asked her on the 20th of April to accept being deprived of the daily apparitions until June 4th. Vicka, who could refuse Our Lady nothing, accepted. It was difficult for her, but even so she remained in perfect joy.

What tests?

Following a method established by the ARPA doctors in 1984, they ran a great number of different tests, which were differentiated, notably cutaneous electrical measurements, the recording of multiple data from a series of polygraphs, one of which could record Marija and Ivan in synchronism. Many psychological tests were administered, particularly the Rorschach and Raven's matrices.

I don't know why an EEG was not run, although a neurologist and a psychiatrist were present. It is nevertheless a key test and we had hoped to repeat it in synchronism with today's equipment which is so much more advanced. It could give us a more precise knowledge of what is going on in the brain, in and out of ecstasy.

The tests ran non-stop for 48 hours. They were quite taxing for the visionaries' patience. 510 different questions were asked. They submitted to them with humor in order to soften the inhumanity of the treatments.

Marija's report

Following Marija's return to Medjugorje on May 3, 1998, Bonifacio recorded her response:

> The study of the ecstasies will bring no more data than that which has already been gathered, but they are hoping to obtain much more from the questions and answers. They asked, for example:
>
> — "When your mother was pregnant with you, did she carry you with joy?"
>
> We did not know how to answer. They wanted to know everything from our childhood to the present time. Vicka was joking, especially when they showed us strange designs and inkblots on a piece of paper and asked us what it represented for us.

— *"Nothing and everything," answered Vicka. "Elephant or mosquito."*

We had a good laugh. If you don't say anything, the psychologists will say that you are not co-operating. So Vicka forced herself to see animals, Ivan saw clouds, and I saw butterflies and flowers. Maybe the doctors were only trying to determine if we have any imagination.

They told my husband:

— *"Your wife has a higher-than-average intelligence."*

They had us play little games, so much so that I said:

— *"What should I think or not think?" I finally retained a bit of logic, seeing as they had an instruction book.*

They measured Vicka's blood pressure for 24 consecutive hours. So she went to bed with that apparatus on her arm. I was dispensed from that test because I had to sleep at home with my little children. The doctors who had placed the cuff of the sphygmomanometer on Vicka's arm for 24 hours had tightened it too much, and suddenly Vicka's arm began to swell and to harden. She asked for the cuff to be removed but was told: "We cannot remove it, but we could loosen it a bit." To which Vicka replied: "Tomorrow I will say: it didn't even let me sleep!"

The next day, they claimed (for they had not left her for a moment):

— *"We saw that you were sleeping perfectly well."*

Vicka retorted:

— *"And I can't even fib about it."*

Those were two very intense days. They tried

to provoke us by rehashing some of the negative comments, especially from priests who didn't believe in the apparitions: "Gospa talks too much, etc." At one point I heard Vicka shouting in the next room and I thought:

— "My God! What's going on? A fight's going to break out".

They later explained:

— "We purposely goaded you in order to provoke a reaction and thus discover your weaknesses." Vicka reacted instantly. They excused themselves and explained that they had to test their reactions.

— "Why didn't you warn me in advance?" asked Vicka.

— "Because if we had warned you, you wouldn't have become angry."

[Editor's note: since the publication of the French edition of *Latest News*, the results of the medical tests on the visionaries have been released; they are published in the appendix, page 220.]

2. VISIT WITH MONSIGNOR PERIC, MARCH 19, 1998

I visited with Monsignor Ratko Peric, Bishop of Mostar, for the first time on March 19, 1998 at 3 p.m. As I had known his predecessor, Bishop Zanic, I had hoped for a long time that I would be invited to visit with him. I had been going about it the wrong way and had concluded that the bishop did not wish to see me.

Bishop Peric

When I went about it the right way, with a clear request transmitted by the parish priest, Father Ivan Landeka, he willingly welcomed me.

In my mind it was a private visit, inspired by respect for his apostolic authority and divine right, as well as wanting to know his authorized point of view first-hand, and taking into account where it was well founded.

I had hoped this visit would remain discreet. Two days later, on March 21st, Bishop Peric courteously faxed me a bulletin he was to publish in the next copy of his *Catholic Information Agency* (Mostar Kiun), in which he described me with these epithets: "naïve, frivolous, incorrect, scandalous, morally inadmissible." The next morning, March 22, I faxed back:

> *I thank you for receiving me. I was happy to get to know you, and to be better informed of your point of view.*
>
> *I considered our meeting to be private and not be the object of an editorial published by your information Agency.*
>
> *It would be regrettable if this communique were published: [...] if it opened up a controversy just as I am trying to achieve the silence you hope for.*

A letter was posted the next day but it was delivered only two months later. In it Bishop Peric maintained his duty to denounce me publicly.

For the sake of truth, which the bishop himself says he values, it is necessary for me here to give my version of that visit. I will do so with all due respect for the bishop and without returning the infamous name-calling with which he described me. I will refrain from reproaching him for the inaccuracies of the text he is spreading against me. He makes me out to be much older than I am. I prefer to explain this as a well-meaning indulgence which can excuse my faults by the inherent senility which comes with old age. I thank him cordially for this.

On the 19th of March, at 3 p.m., I rang the doorbell of the bishop's residence in Mostar. I was astounded to find it in perfect condition, after the fire which had gutted it during the war. It was perfectly renovated, more beautiful than before, a sign of Bishop Peric's efficiency.

As I rang the bell, Mr. Sorin and one of the pilgrims who had accompanied me by car to the bishop's palace joined me. They wanted to pray just before the time of the meeting. The bishop's secretary, a young and handsome Croat, cordially opened the door. He directed us to a waiting room and came for me shortly afterwards for what I thought would be a one-on-one meeting with the bishop. But the secretary remained and took notes. This served to prepare the bulletin against Father Laurentin. The bishop, a good-looking and healthy man began speaking amiably. He mentioned how during his theology classes he had studied Our Lady, using my books, and how he held my works in high esteem before I ever began working on Medjugorje.

This was followed by a courteous exchange, but it was really a dialogue of the deaf. He was preparing his news-report, while I was simply trying to understand him better in a comprehensive exchange, to bring our points of view closer, and to conform to the good order of the diocese, which I had now visited more than thirty times. I wished to focus his attention on the superabundance of graces conferred on Medjugorje by the record number of confessions, conversions and healings. Those spiritual questions, which were outside his sphere of interest, did not enter the heart of the discussion. He kept coming back to the minute, minuscule and marginal reproaches he had methodically prepared, dossier in hand, not on the heart of the matter, but trying to find fault in my opinions on insignificant details, taken not only from my books but from my public comments and my private correspondence. His criticism, which he amiably qualified as "serious," was often based on distortion or incomprehension of my works.

Faced with the senseless and irrelevant mediocrity of most of the subjects launched (news unrelated to the event and grace of Medjugorje), I was in no hurry to answer. The aim of my visit was not to justify myself but to engage in a spiritual dialogue. In that I failed. I was unable to bring about a deep exchange on the basic issues during two to three hours of dialogue.

I will quickly go over, one by one, all the reproaches which became the subject of our conversation, and the information I considered, and a few points that the bishop did not mention in his highly selective summary of the conversation.

Ivan

In 1983 the visionary, Ivan, was taken out of the seminary in Dubrovnik after one year for lack of academic skill. In 1984 I tried to clarify the misunderstanding which had him politely excluded despite his intelligence, his spiritual life, his humanness and his peasant wisdom that I had noticed. This had led to a cordial dialogue with the Dubrovnik Jesuits. They had spontaneously witnessed to his kindness, his obedience and his camaraderie. The problem was academic. I related this briefly in an article for *France Catholique*. It was also published without my knowledge in *Glas Koncila* 5, 1984, p. 7. The article provoked a furor in Croatia, 100 times worse than in France, and awoke a fervor for Medjugorje that many had thought dead and buried. From then on, I was on the communist government's black list, under the initiative of M. Lalik, senior civil servant of Zagreb.

Wanting to maintain peace and good will at all levels (including diplomatic negotiations to appease the communist authorities), I expressed my regrets for having hurt the diocese of Dubrovnik and the esteemed Jesuits. Realizing that the translation of part of an elliptical sentence had been misunderstood, I explained that part to make myself better understood. The bishop holds that explanation against me as a falsification of my original text, as if an author has not the right to explain his thoughts in order to be better understood beyond the ambiguities which are always detrimental to the truth and to personal relations.

But why waste our time on details, which are so far removed from the serious problem of Medjugorje? Why does the bishop constantly seek to divert our attention away from what is essential, as if he didn't want to see it?

Nicolas Bulat

Second reproach: In the second volume of the *Latest News* in 1984, I mentioned that an "expert" on the Commission formed by Bishop Zanic was among those "seeking to have Monsignor Franic removed, and to be replaced by Bishop Zanic." Nothing else. *I didn't give that expert's name,* and reported what an anonymous reliable source from Split had told me. I had met courteously with Nicolas Bulat. My accuser qualifies that clause as "scandalous and morally unacceptable."

What I did not understand very well was how Nicolas Bulat recognized *himself* in this affair, since his name had never been mentioned. Neither did I expose him to defamation like the Bishop of Mostar exposes me openly and shamelessly since 1984. I did not describe that expert with any defamatory remarks such as those levelled at me by Bishop Peric.

The reproach is the following: according to Bishop Peric, Nicolas Bulat wrote to me on two occasions, asking for clarification. I do not remember ever receiving those letters. Mail was irregular in Yugoslavia at the time. If the late priest and theologian, whom I respect, and whom I have cited objectively elsewhere in his interview with Vicka (DN 4, p. 84-86), had wanted a rectification (for which he could have asked me in person when

I went to Split or Medjugorje), I would have told him voluntarily how I had only reported the information I had received from a reliable source, I have neither precise information nor certitude of the implication of Nicolas Bulat, a perfectly honorable priest, in the reported incident. I openly admit that his posthumous rectification must prevail.

But that is once again totally foreign to the debate over Medjugorje. It is one of those petty faults against Laurentin and Medjugorje that aims at demolishing my reputation, since as the saying goes: "*To demolish Medjugorje, one must demolish Laurentin.*"

It is a dreadful thing to be seen as the bull confronting the authority, which is justified *a priori*. In any case, the bull must die and the matador must be glorified. That is the way of the world and sometimes of the Church when it does not know how to live in charity.

Vicka and her diary

Bishop Peric[1] accuses me of being naïve for denying "the existence of Vicka's personal diary" in which she would have written opinions against Bishop Zanic: "He is the cause of all this disorder."

Father Grafenaucr, whom the bishop had received for some time at his home in order to examine the Medjugorje dossier, related this to me. Did Bishop Zanic ever find a page of diary or notes in which this accusation was written? I will refrain from contesting since Bishop Peric affirms it. I have in my possession Vicka's diaries (I am the only informant who enjoys that privilege). In them I have never found that comment.

I do know that Vicka had asked Our Lady during an apparition about the situation concerning the two Franciscans who had been banished and punished, and who had prayed for Our Lady's intervention. I found it regrettable that she had put such a question to Our

Lady, and had brought about such a disagreeable response from those in authority. For the integrity of my information, whose purpose is to keep everything in the open, I objectively exposed this sad affair which I deplored. I inform as a critical observer and not as an unconditional apologist. I have dedicated the first annex of my book, *Message and Teachings of the Virgin of Medjugorje* (p. 310-338) to this end. I literally quoted the words used by the two Franciscans, Ivan and Ivica, which the bishop said he had read in Vicka's diary. Zealous priests, they where devastated by the administrative measure which banished them from the Franciscan Order, relieved them of their vows and suspended them *a divinis* which excluded them from any form of ministry. I did not agree but I deplored that a response from Our Lady had been provoked in a judicial and polemic matter. I ask myself in what manner the Franciscans, judge and jury, had not hardened Vicka's answer. The diary held by Bishop Peric justifies their exactitude.

I also deplored the fact that the two priests' appeal to the supreme tribunal *"Apostolic Signature,"* whose judgement was favorable to them, had been blocked by administrative authorities. It is always regrettable when a government intervenes in the statutory independence of justice (p. 337). I had mentioned it with prudence and care, not wanting to conceal any of the information. It took eight years to break the Church's supreme tribunal deadlock, to be freed from the powers that be, to finally end, and to lift the illegal sanctions. That official dismissal against which the two Franciscans had appealed, only partly explains the negative message Vicka had deemed necessary to transmit on Our Lady's behalf. The comments were regrettable in that they placed the Virgin and the established authorities at odds. But they were not contrary to fundamental truth. The hardening of the authorities on many levels, leading to abuse of power such as that rectified by the Supreme Tribunal, is always regrettable.

Vicka has learned a lot from her error (that is: having Our Lady interfere in local quarrels). She now shrugs it off saying she didn't receive any information from Our Lady concerning the Herzegovina polemic. The illegal sanctions against the two Franciscans are one of the most astonishing pieces in the Herzegovina puzzle.

I am probably wrong in reporting this recent response from Vicka, as it could be taken as a new "lie." The reason I am abandoning the information on Medjugorje is because in such an escalating conflict, it becomes increasingly difficult for the truth to be heard. Concerning my "misinformation," we will see on page 84 where lies the misinformation which boomerangs back to the passionate accuser.

Frivolity

In 1985, according to Bishop Peric, I quoted a pilgrim's letter where the visionaries had recommended reading my books, on Gospa's advice. For purposes of publicity and ridiculous vanity I supposedly propagated this Echo. I had a lot of difficulty in finding the incriminating reference, as the bishop's information was not exact. I finally found the text on another page (DN 3, p. 27) and was surprised because my statement was the opposite of the accusation. I had heard a rumor circulating that a videotape being distributed contained a comment by a visionary, which had Our Lady recommending my books.

Knowing many visionaries, I do not appreciate it when, very rarely, one of them deems it necessary to bestow some praise on me from Our Lady. I always fear such praise might be inspired by an attempt to get into my good graces. I reported the rumor that was circulating merely in order to establish the following:

> *With all due respect to Our Lady and the apparitions, I feel I have no right to use such*

comments as a recognition of authenticity, nor
as an argument in my conflict with the bishop,
etc. (DN 3, p. 27).

It is regrettable that the bishop of Mostar ridicules me and discredits me in such clarifications, which are necessary to cut short any such rumors.

I do not believe that frivolity, vanity, or pretentious ostentation characterize my books, my works or my conduct. If I am wrong, I would willingly attempt to make honorable amends.

Disobedience of the Franciscans

Bishop Peric reproaches me for ignoring (comically) the disobedience of the two Franciscans towards the Pope. In the incriminating passage (DN 4, p. 59-60), I made known Monsignor Franic's mediation to reconcile the bishop and the Franciscans. I noted the first good results as the two Franciscans had written to their General and to Cardinal Ratzinger, asking how they could proceed (towards reconciliation). I was well informed in the matter. I added these words which warranted Bishop Peric's ridicule: *"I regard this case as a true miracle of Medjugorje."*

What I meant by this metaphorical expression is analogous to what St. Augustine said: *"The germination of a grain of wheat is more extraordinary than a miraculous prodigy."* I would welcome it as such a miracle if Bishop Peric, renouncing his canonical destruction of reputations, of vocations and of conversions, entered in the Medjugorje movement of grace to promote a spiritual blossoming and the reconciliation everyone is longing for.

I regret that the bishop qualifies as *"comical"* the sad drama, which is Herzegovina, that fratricidal and destructive conflict. It is never comical when in the Church, the devil's temptations transform fraternal cooperation into a destructive battle. It is sad when the hardening of the law diverts from its objectives in order to banish fervent priests, to deprive them of their canonical mission or to place them in irregular situations which can only lead to their destruction.

Witnessing all the wounds inflicted on so many in Herzegovina, I consider as a spiritual miracle the fact that the vast majority of Franciscans remain respectful of the bishop and are obedient to him, rebuking those who disobey regardless of the fraternal sentiment which binds them to the victims. During the last Chapter of the Franciscans where 190 met together, 130 voted to remain obedient to the bishop. In spite of the huge sacrifices it demanded, they signed the documents confirming their relinquishing of numerous parishes as asked of them, the best of those parishes, whose parishioners, one presumes, will unfortunately not accept this solution. Among the 130 who voted in *favor* were all those who, from near or far, are linked with the events of Medjugorje, concerned as they are with honoring Our Lady's message of peace.

May the authorities understand these miracles of the heart, because an authority that has no heart, even a civil one, cultivates war rather than peace and the common good of all.

From the Pope

Bishop Peric reproaches me for another misinformation. I wrote in *Chrétiens Magazine* #103, P. 35: *"The Pope did not insist"* on making a pilgrimage to Medjugorje, a pilgrimage which he has often clearly and discreetly asked for, but, *"during his trip to Sarajevo, he allowed a large part of his entourage to leave him for a day in order to publicly make a pilgrimage to Medjugorje."*

"It was not his entourage," said Bishop Peric, "but a few reporters and ambassadors." I had used the word "entourage" in a wider sense: those *accompanying the Pope from Rome to Sarajevo*. They were not only reporters and ambassadors, as the press release quoted. There was a bishop (who is one with the Pope in the collegiality defined by the Council), a prelate, representatives of the Secretary of State, and the ambassadors who were accredited to the Holy See. In the direct style, which is typical of magazine reports, I used the word "authorized" in the wider sense. When I reported the news in DN 16, p. 50, I used more rigorous terms. I had no precise information on the conditions under which this group of 11 persons, in various degrees close to the Pope, left him for a day. Can one believe that they did so without being reassured in one way or another that the Pope did not see this as an inconvenience, and that others would make the pilgrimage he was longing to undertake? This fact somehow seems very significant. Bishop Peric is free to interpret the nuances.

In a short and private four line correspondence with a Dutch friend, I answered his pressing questions in short form: *"The hard and crafty action by the bishop, regretted and respected by the Pope, will undoubtedly be fatal to Medjugorje"* (that is, the future of the shrine). That the Pope should respect the local bishop's position, following an unchanging principle of his government, is manifestly evident. That he somewhat privately regrets the constant battle against the spiritually exemplary pilgrimages is often expressed in his high regard for the fruit, and the encouragement he gives bishops who also express a desire to make this pilgrimage. I will say no more, following the principle that one does not embarrass the head of state.

On the testimonies: DN 9, 80-82; 10, 95-96; 12, 38; 13, 51; 14, 45-57; 15, 43-46; 16, 48-50)

The latae sententiae *sanction against Jozo Zovko*

Bishop Peric reproaches me for another misinformation. Apparently I was supposed to have said that he had excommunicated Father Jozo Zovko. I did speak of a sanction in DN 15, p. 34. I reprinted exactly what Bishop Peric had written, that is, that Fra Jozo Zovko would be *"Suspens latae sententiae"* (that is *ipso facto,* and not by a judiciary act). If elsewhere in a simplified magazine style I used the word *"excommunicated"* instead of *"suspens"* (a word misunderstood by the public according to the Larousse dictionary), I willingly correct this pedagogical lapse and refer the reader to the original and rigorous text of DN 15, p. 34.

Fr. Jozo Zovko

My deepest regret is the battle waged by the bishop to discredit the priests, whose fruitful spirituality provoke so many deep conversions. I feel very small in their presence (see below).

I will not go over the "misinformation" of which I am supposedly guilty in my reporting of the judgement by the *Apostolic Signature.* The latter broke up the abuse of power against the two Franciscans, Iva and Ivica (see following p. 84). Does releasing minute, insignificant details, in order to convince his correspondents that I invented these serious matters, serve the truth? Would that my adversary not play the mud slinger who gets slung and exposes himself to the French proverb which is written on the English crown's coat-of-arms: *Honni soit qui mal y pense* (Evil be to him who evil thinks).

What is left unsaid

Bishop Peric presents only a small part of our meeting. He has resumed the passionate accusations established by his predecessor against the first two priests who assumed, under heroic conditions, the defense of the Church and the faithful, and of the faith and the exceptional grace of Medjugorje, and against communist opposition. The first was condemned to a long prison term from which he was released with the help of thousands of Medjugorje pilgrims who petitioned for his release. Why bring up those sordid and inveterate accusations?

Jozo Zovko said: *"They are slander."* As for Tomislav Vlasic whom I have questioned on numerous occasions concerning these accusations, he does not defend himself, but says: *"I refuse to lower myself to those sordid comments. I will let God defend me."* Therefore, I will not expand on the subject.

The bishop believes he also has evidence against Tomislav Vlasic: letters from Manda, an ex-nun who bore a priest's child. She is raising the child in a neighboring country. I had already examined this accusation at the time Bishop Zanic was proclaiming it proudly in front of three visionaries who because of it, turned away in various degrees from planned vocations (DN 5, p. 50-53). I mention diverse problems which cause one to doubt the massive proof constituted by those letters:

Fr. Tomislav Vlasic

1. Manda's letters kept by the bishop are of different handwriting. This would be remarkable for one person.

2. On December 26, 1985, Manda wrote a tough protest letter to the bishop, (DN 5, p. 53): *"That supposed letter of mine which is deposited in your case file, is not from me,"* etc.

It is regrettable how much importance is given to these accusations and defamation in the battle against Medjugorje and the people who serve this great cause. They are aimed at persons whose spiritual and humane action, as with Jozo Zovko, are amply and internationally recognized. *Even if* they had committed some fault in the past, if that fault had been atoned for by a perfectly edifying lifestyle, why would one wish to cling to such morose delight? Why wish the death of the sinner and not welcome the prodigal son? Why govern contrary to the Gospels by returning (like a dog after its vomit) to the ambiguous accusations whose proof is debatable? Can defamation be a means of governing in Jesus Christ's Church?

I was more interested by what the bishop told me of his actions against the Franciscans of his diocese. They had a flourishing novitiate. That novitiate is now closed.[2] The Franciscans who represent the majority of priests in the diocese (more than 200) are condemned to dying out. Considering their spirituality, this insidious, undermining process is most regrettable. The closing of the Franciscan novitiate in the province of Herzegovina, preceded by the refusal of all canonical missions for the young priests formed in this novitiate during the preceding years, creates a serious shortage, not only for peace, but for spiritual action and the very future of the Church. Is it normal for 42 priests of the diocese to be technically retired, to the detriment of pastoral tasks being unfulfilled, as well as to their psychic, moral and priestly equilibrium?

At the end of my visit with him, Bishop Peric asked me to stop writing on Medjugorje in order to facilitate his episcopal government. Ever mindful of obeying the bishop's decision, I told him that I could not stop this volume from being published because I was already irreversibly committed, but *"upon your request, I will firmly make this sacrifice and will confirm it officially as soon as the decision is formally taken."*

I thought that this sacrifice and deference on my part would also bring about peace on his part. Unfortunately, the accusing document of March 21st has not confirmed my hopes. Moreover, the accompanying letter was like a courteous declaration of war:

> *Yesterday's meeting suggests to me that I should prepare a book of solid denials on the non-truths you have published on Medjugorje over the years (...) I deeply regret having to take this severe action against you.*

Why did he deem it necessary to provoke with threats what I had already granted by deference and understanding, threats to which I have always been immune, including when I faced Nazi and communist tribunals? Bishop Peric, in his letter posted on March 24, and which I received on May 15th, informed me of his resolute actions against me in Rome (from which I had already experienced the effects):

> *I do not content myself with publicizing your deplorable information. I regularly inform the Dicastery (court of justice) of the Holy See.*

Bishop Peric is not a man who knows how to quit. His approach to battles is the exploitation of success, thus the destruction of my reputation. In spite of the hardening of the slander against me, I continue to respect the man for the function and the person who is the Bishop of Mostar. Because threats have never broken me down, I decided without any hesitation, to persevere in my resolve of which I had informed him, hoping that my loyalty and my correct attitude will finally serve the cause of peace, be it at my expense.

Is it hoping for too much? One must always hope, and have faith in the Church and its authority. During the Council, many friends had accused me of being naïve for wanting to meet with Cardinal Ottaviani following the slanders which had brought reprisals against me within the *Theological Commission of the Congregation* and even in the very offices of the Congregation. I waited for the end of the Council to obtain this interview in order not to hamper its work. I applaud myself for meeting with Cardinal Ottaviani, who had distributed pamphlets against my work in the Theological Commission where I worked as an expert, a pamphlet against Laurentin. His greeting was that of a man of heart and truth. He had verified the accusations leveled against me: notably that I was working as an enemy of Our Lady, and that I was an informer for *Fesquet* and *Le Monde*. He told me in his own words:

— "Everything has been clarified. You have worked as a good theologian and a good reporter."

He proposed the redress for which I could have wished. I answered him:

— *"Your faith in me is all I need."*

In short, if I appreciated meeting cordially with Bishop Peric, a strong bishop, capable in his toughness, my regret is that I was not able to interest him in spiritual things, which seems to be so fundamental in the Church. I ardently hope that what comes next will allow me to maintain for him a high esteem which my meetings with Cardinal Ottaviani have established, even after such unfortunate developments.

In the end, only God and Our Lady will be able to appease the constantly escalating fight against Medjugorje. But will they want to? Mary was not able to save her Son from death in spite of her maternal heart. In 1431, Heaven was not able to save Joan of Arc from the arm of the Church system, which is fearsome even when it shoots at the wrong target.

Contrary to all the apparitions that have taken place in the communist world since 1917, Medjugorje was not crushed by the infallible steamroller of Marxism. Medjugorje can still be destroyed by the authority of the Church, if the local bishop persists in the present hardening of his convictions. It is not for fear of threats that I am walking away. My reputation has now been destroyed; I have nothing else to lose. It is only out of respect for the authorities, and abandonment to God, that I am renouncing my work in information, which could hardly continue without being reduced to polemics. Polemics very quickly deteriorate and become vile.

— Chapter 4 —
OPPONENTS

This chapter is a continuation of the preceding one. The local bishop is opposed to Medjugorje and supplies objections in various forms to the opponents against her. Amongst the newest and most influential opponents is Joachim Bouflet, a competent expert in canonization causes. He found an important forum against Medjugorje in an issue of *Famille Chrétienne*. While working with the Roman Congregation for canonization causes, which he does with skill and competence, he unilaterally upholds the point of view of the authorities against Medjugorje, but without attaching much importance to discernment of the fruit. Nevertheless his opinion as a specialist is greatly respected. As is the norm, he benefits from all official support even though he has not looked at all the evidence exhaustively.

The other noted opponent is a Flemish reporter, insatiable informer and a pugnacious expert in news scoops. He had made 24 pilgrimages to Medjugorje when he suddenly made a complete turn around following a three-hour conversation with Bishop Peric. The bishop's arguments (although often presented prudently) are developed to their most extreme viciousness: Medjugorje is the brain-child of Father Tomislav Vlasic who wanted to create a pseudo-sanctuary in Medjugorje based on the model of Hrasno (40 kilometers south-west of Medjugorje).

Medjugorje is most certainly the greatest hoax of the 20th century in the history of the Catholic Church. Satan himself comes, clothed as an angel of light (2 Cor. 11, 14-15) [...] Everything focuses on power, money, and even sex, and has led to disobedience, lies and rebellion against Rome.

How can a fervent and active pilgrim of Medjugorje come to make such an about-face? It is the price for his generous, complete and excessive temperament, which leads to radical rejections after great fervor.

Too many believe in the apparitions as an absolute, whereas they are relative signs given in clear but obscure terms to more or less fragile visionaries. Those absolute believers idealize everything, and believe that the slightest stain, the slightest weakness on the part of a visionary, discredits the whole event. That is how he went (out of a concern for honesty which he honors) from his ardent faith to a viciousness without concession, seeking evil everywhere with refined sharpness. I will reiterate the principal objections, though often repetitive, of these passionate adversaries and that of the constellation of American and British opponents without rehashing those with which I have already dealt in preceding books.

"Apparitions ended, but maintained by mimicry"

It has been repeated for years: the apparitions have ended, but the visionaries just coast along with the acquired momentum, activating reflexes from the past.

I have asked myself that question for some of the visionaries; I tried to reason it out. I was not able to obtain more scientific data, and regretted Jacov's radical refusal, and the tepid response from the rest of the group, to run a new series of tests which could answer some of the objections. Recently, a group of Italian doctors managed to run some of these tests which were done as I was preparing this book. The results were not ready when we went to press, but there did not seem to be any surprises forthcoming. [See p. 220]

Everything seems quite normal for those who have the opportunity to observe the apparitions in public or in private on a regular basis; for Jacov and Vicka who usually have private apparitions, the information gathered from observers is less precise, but nevertheless positive.

The latest medical tests (April 22-23, 1998) have so far revealed that nothing has changed which might call into question the character of the ecstasies.

Visionaries' faux-pas

For more than 15 years, the visionaries have been reproached for errors arising from difficult or near impossible situations.

"Lies"?

The first two visionaries, Ivanka and Mirjana, held back for some time the fact that they were not only going to listen to some tapes that day, but were actually planning to go and smoke some of the tobacco which they threaded all day long with their families.

Each one of us keeps some personal details to oneself. We prefer them to remain private. Is it equitable for someone to denounce their slowness in revealing everything, or their keeping such details to themselves, and then make a drama of it and declare: "They are liars, everything is false at Medjugorje."? Is this a just discernment?

Ivan's deception

Ivan Dragicevic was a timid and introverted child, so much so that his father used to have to drive him over to play with other children. He was severely tried on May 9, 1982, when two members of the Commission came and ordered him to put down in writing the "sign" announced by Our Lady: the third sign which would be given when the apparitions ceased. Having received it under the seal of secrecy, the other five visionaries had refused to co-operate. But Ivan was isolated in the little Franciscan seminary. He felt misunderstood, ill at ease with his studies, and had been threatened with expulsion (which came about one month later). Intimidated by the two commissioners who were mandated by the bishop, he cracked. Left alone with a sheet of paper and an envelope which he was to seal until the day the secret was to be realized, he fretted and paced up and down until he found a very peasant way of saying without saying. What he wrote was so vague that in his mind he figured he had not "written anything." This is what he told me in all sincerity.

By reporting his comments, I unwillingly caused him moral anguish. Fortunately the incident was for him an opportunity to grow in wisdom.

Having heard his declaration, members of the Commission came back and said to him: "Since you have written nothing, we can open the letter." He realized once the envelope was opened that in actual fact he had written something. He had forgotten, and lost face, not only with the members of the commission but also with the parish priests and the other visionaries. Following a grueling meeting with the Commission on March 7, 1985, Father Slavko Barbaric convened the six visionaries in order to ascertain Ivan's veracity as a visionary. The other five confirmed his position as a visionary, all the while reprimanding him for his error. During the days to come, he would weep bitterly. But he did learn from the experience.

> *'It is an error,' concluded Bishop Franic, but he did not write anything on the subject, and in that sense he could say that he had not*

written anything. There is nothing secret on that paper. The other visionaries would confirm that statement (Communication of April 17, 1983).

I explained that situation in DN 4, p. 17-23. I do not need to pursue it. That Ivan's error led some to doubt him is normal, but any man, any visionary, and even any saint can make an error without affecting what is essential. Why turn such incidents into mountains?

Our Lady against the Bishop?

Vicka was reproached for having questioned Our Lady about the two Franciscans: Ivan Prusina and Ivica Vego. I openly deplored it, and blamed the two priests for demanding insistently that Vicka submit their case to Gospa. As a rule, the visionaries are more careful, and refuse to ask Our Lady indiscreet questions which are not their responsibility and are beyond the scope of the messages. But the two priests, having been supended from their priestly faculties, as well as their vows of poverty, chastity and obedience purely because of administrative measures, demanded to be judged according to the law. But the turning of the wheels of justice was stopped by administrative authority. This ordeal was destroying their faith, their priesthood and their confidence in the Church. Vicka felt sorry for them.

If Vicka had no right to question Gospa on the matter, can we condemn her for having tried to support those young priests in need, and to give them consolation which supported them during their long desert crossing, prolonged beyond measure by depriving them of Church law?

I have agreed with the most severe criticism for a long time, out of respect we must have for authority. However, Vicka's answer did prove to be accurate when the Church's Supreme Court dismissed the sanctions against the two priests 11 years later on March 27, 1993. The sanctions were declared null, and contrary to Church law. One can read the text and the discussion of this painful affair in *"Medjugorje and the Teachings of Our Lady of Medjugorje"* p. 319-337, and the definitive conclusion of the tribunal in *"Signature Apostolique"* DN 13, p. 47-49. In a text accompanied by the Bishop's seal, the chancellor of Mostar seems to contest what was just said. I quote him with all respect:

Misinformation

Laurentin is spreading misinformation, and publishes facts which are not true, causing a veritable storm in Medjugorje. It is not true that the Apostolic Signature Tribunal delivered the judgement of "six Cardinals," including the "dean of the Sacred College," which "re-instated" the two Franciscan priests. The dean of the Sacred College did not sign the verdict, and there were not six signatures. We realize how Laurentin did not have the text in hand and had at best caught a glimpse of it or read it superficially.

— The supreme judges of the *Apostolic Signature* were in fact 5 and not 6 as I specified myself in DN 13, p. 49. But Bishop Peric did not read it. I do not know where he got this tid-bit, but numbers do not change anything.

— Cardinal Gantin, the first signature on the document was *not yet* dean of the Sacred College at the time of his signature. Monsignor Peric has a point on this chronological precision. Monsignor Gantin signed document #17907/86 on March 27, 1993 and became dean June 5th of the same year. I mentioned his title, which was his when we went to print. As for the rest, these details do not for one minute erase the fact that the abuse of authority committed against those two priests was censured and rebuked by the Supreme Court with the signature of five Cardinals including the future dean of the Sacred College. To state that the information is without basis is to mislead the audience. To treat it as spreading "misinformation" is akin to trial by personal opinion. The communiqué given with the Bishop's seal is contrary to the truth in so far as it declares that the Supreme Court trial which nullified the administrative measures against the two Franciscans is a misinformation of Laurentin's, and that the latter did not see the judgement in question. So, the misinformation is not where one is supposed to think it is! Let the mudslinger be splashed.

The two priests had appealed the illegal administrative measure taken against them. They asked to be judged and promised to submit to that judgement. Not only were they not heard, but when they did manage to present their case to the *Apostolic Signature* tribunal, that trial itself was put on hold for many years by an administrative authority on a very high level who had ordered the two Franciscans to submit to the original sanctions.

It is a very serious matter when the operation of a Supreme Court of Justice is halted in order to cover up its guilty authorities. In any country, this becomes a matter of state. In Rome this is an even graver situation as the Supreme Court of Justice is not the affair of civil servants. The judges of the Supreme Court are Cardinals in whom we entrust the government of the Church.

I have reported the fact very discreetly, without naming the persons directly responsible in order not to create scandal. But what is most stupefying is the fact that the one who was responsible for bringing the trial to a stop was later named Prefect of that very tribunal. This created a delicate situation, and that is why the Pope transferred that Prefect to another post after only three years. He usually nominates people to such positions for a much longer period of time. That is how the trial was allowed to reopen, to do justice to the truth. It would be regrettable if the conflict persisted and forced me to reveal the rest.

It is a fact that one of the two Franciscan priests gave up the priesthood in 1988. The Chancellor of the diocese of Mostar reported this in his letter of September 15, 1997, entitled: *Rene Laurentin's Misinformation* (The letter was addressed to Mrs. R.C. with the bishop's seal). It is the very shock wave created by this injustice which unsettled him; I will not dwell on this heart-breaking consequence of the abuse of power. It is a pity that the bishop shows no regret but rather the satisfaction of discovering another flaw in a Franciscan. It is regrettable that these long years of conflict have pushed him to these limits. It is a fact that Bishop Zanic has maintained the ban on all canonical missions for Fra Ivan Prusina, the priest who persevered in his vocation. The bishop intervened (before the judgement of the Supreme Court), in the diocese of Dubrovnik, asking the local bishop to dismiss him. It is always regrettable when judicial and canonical measures place sincere men and priests in unbalanced situations. Fra Ivan Prusina had to go into exile in order to escape irreversible persecution. I cannot find any joy in this. Again I ask: where is the misinformation?

Why do those presently with Episcopal authority emphasize with delight the fact that, despite their judicial wrong, the priest who remained faithful throughout his ordeal continues to be banned from exercising his priestly faculties in the diocese of Mostar?

Is the shrine of Medjugorje recognized?

This is another misinformation held against me: I apparently reported that the shrine of Medjugorje was recognized. Would that not be an absurd invention because in those places where supernatural apparitions are not recognized, all official pilgrimages are prohibited?

Well, no. Some non-recognized apparitions have become recognized pilgrimage sites in the Church. That is the case for the Rue du Bac, where Pope John-Paul II went officially as a pilgrim.

That nuance is noted in the *"Criteria to Judge Apparitions"* published in 1978 by Cardinal Seper. To answer ambiguities and confusions of the past, this document states that the actions of a bishop in cases of apparitions should be twofold:

1. Instead of standing back as many did, he should quickly discern the facts, and if nothing opposes it, allow some public manifestations of the cult and devotion, keeping watch over the events with great prudence. This is the equivalent of the formula: *nihil obstat* — for now, no obstacle.

2. With the passage of time, and the experience of the spiritual fruit born of this new devotion, if possible, to pass supernatural judgement on the truth.

Under these conditions, the first thing to do is to acknowledge the cult (to watch over it, to assume responsibility, and direct the pilgrimages as Cardinal Kuharic had planned). Then one could go on to recognize the authenticity of the apparitions. The second step is not even necessary to the survival of a shrine, as we see in so many sanctuaries.

Once again the misinformation does not come from me, but is part of a concerted effort over the years to destroy me in the eyes of the public, by the bishops and by Rome where Bishop Peric sends reports against me. His predecessor accused me, after my very first book in 1984, of writing for money (I supposedly made one million dollars from it), of having asked him to lie, and of having succumbed to the seduction of the visionaries rather than to the authority of the bishop (DN 2). I regret these persistent attacks against my reputation, which do not befit the relationship between any two persons, much less between two Christians. When those who slander my name state that, because I do not respect the bishop, then in turn I do not deserve to be respected, I answer that I do respect the bishop. I even wrote in DN 2 an article full of praise for Bishop Zanic, because I not only respect the Monsignor's function as a bishop, but his person, and his qualities. Bishop Zanic was a man of heart, even if his impulses have led him to make even worse mistakes than those held against me by many, in large part trivialities or distortions of my comments.

I placed those comments, not in the chapter on the Magisterium, but in the chapter on the opponents who convey the same objections usually coming from the same source. I nevertheless hold Bishop Peric in high esteem. I respect him as a courteous and intelligent man, gifted with great talents. My only regret is that the exercise of his canonical power seems to close his eyes to the spiritual side, which is of paramount importance in the Church. I pray with all my heart that he might overcome his human limitations, just as I pray I might overcome my own of which I hope to be aware.

Vicka is besieged

I will now deal in greater detail with another minor incident, seeing the importance Bishop Peric, Waterinck and others are attaching to it. They accuse Vicka of obtaining a pseudo-revelation from Our Lady in favor of a commercial venture, in complicity with Father Slavko.

I was reproached for having kept it hidden in DN 16. The fact is I did not attach much importance to this minor and private incident. Moreover, the incident had taken place in the spring of 1995, and I did not receive the full details until that summer. I will refrain from mentioning names out of respect for those involved.

Some benefactors (let's call them B.) of Medjugorje were asked in March of 1995 to finance the construction of a *Pastoral Centre* in Medjugorje, in fact a 100 bed hotel with a chapel for pilgrims. Vicka was supposed to have said to the promoters, "Our Lady wants this hotel."

When Father Slavko got news of this accusation against the visionary, he immediately denied that Gospa could have intervened in a financial and commercial matter:

> *"That does not come from Gospa," he answered B. quickly, without taking the time to consult Vicka.*

Then B. received a fax from Vicka, confirming that the Mother of God had given her consent and insisted that they begin the construction.

B. once again questioned Father Slavko and received this answer: "That benefactor frequently insisted that Vicka question Our Lady on the construction." Weary of this persistence, she finally asked and got this vague answer:

— "Gospa said we *can* begin constructing."

We "can," not *"I request it!"*

Fr. Slavko Barbaric

Slavko asked Vicka why she had kept this discussion from him.

— "I didn't dare speak about it in front of my father. I was annoyed by B.'s insistence," she said essentially.

She apologized in writing for having given an apparently negative response to Father Slavko.

— "It happened, it won't happen again," she concluded, in some confusion.

A fax from Slavko dated April 3, 1995 adds this further clarification:

After having read the letter, I knew for a fact that the text did not come from Vicka [...] She was preparing for a trip to Rome and had little time. Mr. B. and his son prepared the text and asked Vicka to rewrite it in her own handwriting. She did it so hurriedly. But only the last sentence was Vicka's, that is, the greetings. Vicka shed many tears over the matter and apologized repeatedly.

It is not right to involve Our Lady and the visionaries in worldly matters [...] Vicka is very gracious and does not want to send anyone away. She does too much for pilgrims. Her home is constantly besieged. She prays for the sick, receiving them night and day. She often collapses from fatigue. When someone comes, as did B.'s family, asking for the support of his interests, blunders occur. [...] That does not put Vicka's credibility in doubt in my mind [...] What you do with your money must not depend on anything else other than your own conscience and decision [...] I regret this incident. (Fax dated April 3rd).

One of Slavko's correspondents is stunned that Vicka, educated by Our Lady for a period of 14 years, would still lie in such an insignificant matter (fear of her father's reprisal rather than fear of sin). Shouldn't apparitions prevent such types of blunders?

It seems to me rather exaggerated to be speaking of lies; Vicka, put on the spot, answered with a vague denial to appease both Slavko and her father — as one does to escape from a thorny situation. Who among us has not performed such verbal acrobatics when placed in a delicate position?

Curious epilogue: In May, Slavko (who had not answered the fax by the end of April, decided to intervene, *"not in the name of Our Lady but in his own name."* The builders of the hotel, "an honest family in whom we can place our trust," are facing difficult financial times. "If possible, it would be appropriate to help them."

The Medjugorje adversary who published this report concludes:

This dossier proves that Vicka and Slavko Barbaric are deceiving the people in asking them when they ask for money for the hotel that family B. wants to build in Medjugorje.

No, Vicka's generous availability was abused. A vague response was obtained from her. She was asked to copy it in her own handwriting, tired though she was. And she rushed because of her departure. Slavko and Vicka have always insisted on the eventual donor's freedom to act.

The matter is complex and must be taken in context with Vicka's dedication in life and the psychology of the Mediterranean mentality. Vicka, always giving of herself and concerned with helping all those who work for a good cause, acceded to the insistent requests of some good Christians involved in a financial situation beyond their financial capabilities. Their backs to the wall, they went out of their way to find help. Confronted by their predicament, Vicka came to their rescue with encouraging but circuitous words which resembled escape hatches, rather than lies. About to leave on a hectic trip, the petitioners managed to have her recopy what they had written, a synopsis of what they had recalled from her encouraging words. Vicka had almost forgotten this incident where her kind heart had led her too far afield.

When Father Slavko was notified, he did not mince his words. Vicka repented and wept bitterly.

As for Slavko, he has not stopped telling the benefactor that he is free to do as he pleases with his money, and that Our Lady does not intervene in such matters. He did not try to hide Vicka's ambiguous answers; he even set them in excessive contrast, to the amiable and encouraging style of speech which is common to Vicka and many of those who ask for her intercession. As for Vicka, she usually deals with petitioners sensibly, with a good heart and a flavor of wit that I very much admire. She sometimes falls into traps and she regrets it. Such is the case here.

All day long Vicka is pestered with all sorts of demands and sometimes even abusive ones. Occasionally she refuses them, but always with an amiable smile. She answers the crowds quickly and clearly, though they hardly give her a chance to breathe. But she helps them, consoles them, and encourages them to pray. How is she able to answer all of these demands so quickly, including those of well-intentioned but self-seeking people? In such cases, she repeats half-baked all-encompassing formulae trying to doing her best.

There have been occasions when I chided her for answering too quickly. It is impossible for anyone, no matter who, even a visionary, to be absolutely perfect: for fear of losing all credibility in their mission and their witnessing. The visionaries are fragile beings as we all are, challenged by a rather difficult way of life. Moreover, Vicka lives in deep personal holiness, giving all she has to give. There are dreadful hardships behind that perpetual smile. It is easy to shoot down the weakness in her life while she is constantly exposed to the double fear of either not doing enough or of doing too much. In short, the accusations are excessive, and the basis for them are miniscule and marginal. I am amazed that more serious charges have not sprung up and more frequently. I regret the time lost in such empty debates.

A word about other objections.

Distressing accusations

The present Bishop maintains his predecessor's accusations against the morals of the first two parish priests of Medjugorje: Jozo Zovko, who skillfully directed the deep conversion of the divided parish, and Tomislav Vlasic, his successor since the 15th of August, 1981, who was the guide to an extraordinary spiritual blossoming which profoundly moved those who witnessed it.

It is a widely-known strategy that when one wants to destroy a priest, one accuses him about his morals. It was a common occurrence under the communist regime. It also happens elsewhere because of jealousy or rivalry. I know the case of priests, accused of solicitation in the confessional, who lived in suspension from further spiritual duties for the rest of their natural lives who are not allowed to challenge the slanderous accusations held against them by perpetrators who could not be revealed to them. Bishop Zanic has most likely gathered complaints which might have been sincere but which stemmed from the ambiguity of Father Jozo Zovko's strong 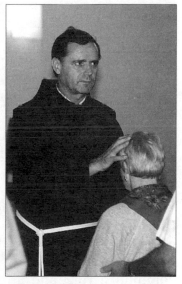 personality. If Fr. Jozo has charisms, they have blossomed from natural gifts. That might explain why, when he lays hands on people, so many fall in that total physical, psychic and spiritual relaxation we call *"Resting in the Spirit."* Others may receive that infilling of the Spirit in a more equivocal manner and that is perhaps why Jozo Zovko more than ever, asks other priests who accompany the pilgrims to lay hands. The numbers then are much fewer.

Bishop Peric showed me the file on Tomislav Vlasic with his usual assurance, but did not allow me to make a photocopy. I refer you back to what I said previously concerning my visit with Bishop Peric (p. 74).

Is this conflict worthy of the Church? The Church is not a place of defamation; it does not seek the death of the sinner, but his conversion, which brings about more joy in heaven than the perseverance of 99 just souls. The Church washes dirty linen under the seal of secrecy in the confessional. Nothing can lift this seal. It is hard to comprehend the spiteful and morose delight, which lingers over these matters. Whatever the faults may be, they would quickly be resolved through charity. This would be easy, as we are dealing with priests who have been instrumental in bringing about more conversions and vocations than 99% of the clergy, including me.

Fr. Leonard Orec

A third Medjugorje parish priest, Father Orec, was accused, not for his morals, which are without reproach but for having built an altar outside the church. The altar was quite necessary for the tens of thousands of pilgrims. A basilica would be necessary to contain just a fraction of these crowds, but that was impossible under communist rule, and afterwards the Bishop's. Would it not be logical that in Medjugorje, as in Lourdes and other pilgrimage sites, we separate the parish functions from the hospitality offered pilgrims? We should then authorize the necessary buildings to accommodate them in the best interests of the faithful and give them the pastoral assistance which they fervently seek in Medjugorje.

For such a construction, which he quickly built when communism was beginning to show signs of weakening,

Father Orec was prohibited from any canonical mission in the diocese. When will they cease the destructive use of *Canon Law* as a weapon to demolish instead of building? Can we return to the Gospel, to reconciliation in charity, the only possibility for an authentic Christianity?

An awkward intrusion: the Franciscan-diocesan conflict

The accusations against Medjugorje are constantly entangled in the conflict between the Bishop and the Franciscans. The Medjugorje problem has nothing to do with that conflict except that the Franciscan pastors demonstrate exemplary conduct amidst impossible conditions. This conduct has garnered Medjugorje a prestige which an enemy might be tempted to tarnish. It is the common ground of the opponents: to attribute to Medjugorje the grievances held against a few Franciscan extremists. It is undeniable that there exists a regrettable conflict between the secular clergy and the Franciscans, which goes back more than 50 years. On June 6, 1975 Pope Paul VI decided to transfer eight Franciscan parishes to secular priests. The application of that decree *Romanis Pontificibus* has never been accepted for the following reasons:

— The authoritarian measures were taken without a true dialogue, which has led to frustrations and mistrust.

— The Franciscans have been complaining for a long time: "What we abandoned was quickly taken. What we asked for in compensation was not respected."

Two things have complicated the problem, which needed more diplomacy and, above all, charity.

1. For hundreds of years, the priests in the region were almost exclusively Franciscans, notably during the persecutions by the Muslim Turks until the end of the last century. This created between the population and the Franciscans a bond, and a synergy of those who were

persecuted endlessly. During the persecutions, the Franciscans, riskily disguised, visited the families as *maternal* uncles. This was done to cover the difference in names (there is a special word in the Croatian language to designate a maternal uncle). The quasi-family relationship which developed remains to this day. When Franciscans are removed from a good parish, it is heart-wrenching for the villagers. They resist. They board-up the church, etc. They react like a child whom we try to separate from his parents. They are assuredly wrong. It is not canonically defendable. But why is there no attempt to ensure a smooth transition, to prepare minds and hearts? In such cases, any good governing body should practise dialogue and diplomacy to ensure a harmonious solution.

What complicates the situation even more is when the evicted priests, or any Franciscan, see members of their flock deprived of the sacraments. They feel obligated to administer the sacraments of baptism, confession and matrimony in order to ensure their spiritual survival. This action brings about their suspension and expulsion from the Franciscan order. The sanctions are justified under the Law, but could the problems not be resolved without leaving so many bodies in the street? When Bishop Peric annexed the Franciscan parishes around Mostar, the Croatians wrongfully kidnapped him. No one was able to stop them, except for the Franciscans, I am told. It was heartbreaking for the priests who opposed those who wanted to maintain family ties with them. But have we thanked them for it?

2. A second factor, just as noble, plays against the Franciscans who have known resistance for many centuries: four centuries of clandestine living under the Turks, and 40 years of communist oppression.

Confronted by difficulties from inside the Church, many have found their old resistance reflexes. They are surely wrong to give in to such behavior, but in the State as in the Church, we recognize those reflexes and avoid provoking them. The problem is that in Herzegovina one cultivates provocation, sure of oneself, especially since it is exercised under the Pope's authority. Should not the Pope's authority be exercised with the heart and the spirit of the Pope, who is directed by charity? Is it not that very same charity which should solve all problems rather than an authoritarian escalation and canonical punishments?

It is a question we cannot help asking when we find Medjugorje artificially involved in this negative escalation which seems to have no other goal than the annihilation of the Franciscan province of Mostar. For centuries it proved to be a heroic, most populated and most deeply spiritual of the Franciscan provinces. It has deep, living roots for the inhabitants. For many years now, young Franciscan priests have received no canonical mission from the bishop of Mostar, and those remaining are more or less irregulars. The novitiate was closed — a program leading to the extinction of the Franciscans in Herzegovina. Is this extinction of vocations and deeply rooted priestly zeal the best and most opportune way of solving the problems of the Church? I will not say any more about this sad matter. There, as in other historical problems, rights and guilt are somehow equally shared. Oh, that we might recognize this in humility, which is inspired by love!

As a rule, today's Church knows how to do this with greatness of soul and humility. With respect to the eastern schism, fruit of the authoritarianism born of Cardinal Humbert, Pope Paul VI and the Council recognized our share of the guilt. Pope Paul VI came to kiss the feet of the Metropolitan, representative of the Patriarch of Constantinople, during a visit to the Sistine Chapel, in repentance for this heart-rending act of the past. We have begged forgiveness from Jews for centuries of anti-semitism and Pope John-Paul II has to date (according to an Italian reporter) publicly asked forgiveness 105 times for errors committed by the Church over the last 2,000 years. He is doing so in order to purify the Church as we approach the millennium. Why could not a request for mutual forgiveness be sought more easily in the Church of Herzegovina? Forgetting the past is often necessary to build the future.

It is by this means that the different hamlets of Medjugorje, mired in deep conflicts, which had often led to deaths, begged each other's forgiveness in July of 1981, in the church. From then on, they have learned to work together once again. It is on such basis that we could find the peace Our Lady is asking for, putting aside battles and ever-degrading conflicts, in order to consecrate all our energies to what is spiritual.

What I appreciate the most in Medjugorje is the fact that you do not hear anything being said about these quarrels, in spite of the pain and frustration experienced by so many. One day a Franciscan from Mostar was updating me on the conflicts, which were going on in the city. Father Pavic, one of the parish priests severely reproached me and asked us to be silent. It didn't matter how well founded the information was. For in Medjugorje, only the spiritual is important. That is how the legitimate church government should try, not to demobilize and extinguish, but to promote the essential, which is flowering in this oasis of peace.

Confusion between the Herzegovina affair and the grace of Medjugorje

In light of the debate, and in deference to Our Lady, it is hoped that the Bishop of Mostar refrains from mixing the accusations against Medjugorje with the conflict against the Franciscans, because Medjugorje has nothing to do with it, except for quite accidental interference. The Franciscan pastoral work in the region is exemplary but impossible in all regards. It is thus regrettable that the full weight of the conflict regarding the takeover of eight parishes by secular priests be laid on their shoulders. It is not their concern. The parish of Medjugorje is not among those being reclaimed by the bishop, as claimed by some. This is not the place to dwell on that regrettable conflict. The Franciscans are in agreement with the transfer of other parishes called for by the Pope.

They only regret that such transfers are being accomplished without dialogue. From parish to parish (from Goude to Mostar and today to Capljina), parishioners do not understand and do not accept the separation from their fathers in faith. For them it is a family uprooting. They wall-up the church (inside back cover), and beg the Franciscans not to leave them deprived of the sacraments of baptism, matrimony, or Holy Mass. It is heart-wrenching for those who are their spiritual fathers. That is how one of the two Franciscans who left in obedience to the bishop, came back to Capljina. Thus the cycle of irregularities and sanctions grows inextricably in a Balkan climate more comparable to the Serbian-Kosovo conflict than to fraternal relationships which are normally those of the Church. Even our modern democracies know how to avoid these situations of inextricable conflicts.

It is not a matter of approving the disobedience of Capljina, where after 18 months, the exiled priests brought in a mysterious bishop whose name and origin they hid so that he might give the sacrament of confirmation.

It is hoped that true spiritual mediators be mobilized to ensure that the transfer of new parishes to secular priests does not bring about new disorders to the detriment of faith, morality and the very life of the Church.

I am thinking of spiritual mediators, on which I insist, to prepare the transition. The present method, which is based on massive authoritarian decisions (followed by sanctions and slander) used against the Franciscans, leave them torn between obedience to the bishop and their traditional flock.

Over the last 40 years, most of them struggled with their spiritual sons in order to force them to respect the authorities. In the end this struggle is leaving them unhappy and isolated between their spiritual sons and the authorities who do not seem to appreciate their efforts.

What complicates matters even more is the fact that the province of Mostar is deprived of its normal government. Each visit from the Franciscan General reminds them of this. The last visit was on November 15th in Mostar.

The complete normalization of our province is suspended. Our province has not held a chapter since 1976. You presently have only an "interim" government. (Speech from the Franciscan General to the province of Herzegovina, 4th November, 1996, p. 17-19).

The situation is analogous to that of a city which had not held elections for 20 years and whose mayor had been named "after consultation" by the government. It would then be very difficult for the said mayor, nominated under such conditions, to bring his rebellious administration in line, many being deprived of their normal rights, or punished with sanctions, which are considered as the authority's best means.

I believe in the Church's authority, but it is difficult to recognize it when it is not in line with the Gospel: understanding and dialogue inspired by charity.

An expert's discernment

Professor Adalbert Robic of the *Faculty of Catholic Theology in Zagreb*, a well known Croatian academic personality, gave this answer to *Globus*, reprinted by *Echo* 136, 5c, to the question: How could the matter of Herzegovina's Franciscans and that of the attitude of the official structures of the Church towards Medjugorje be settled?

This is my personal position. In Herzegovina, both sides need a better sense of divine realities. The Franciscans have accomplished an enormous task for the people throughout its long history. This needs to be recognized. They have been the guardians of the Catholic faith in this part of the world, and have always been on the side of the people. To this day, they are called "uncles", because they truly are part of the Herzegovina family. Why destroy all of this, especially by force, decrees, punishments and threats? Believe me, this is not in the Spirit of Christ or of the Gospel.

Medjugorje is a gift from God to the people of this region. I will make no comment as to the authenticity of the apparitions. [...] But Medjugorje is a place that belongs to God. I had been there a few times as a government employee during the war. Medjugorje is a spiritual oasis where one experiences the nearness of God, as on Mount Sinai. You experience something there that you do not feel in Lourdes or Fatima. That is why people come here from all over the world.

But why do certain priests and bishops see it differently? It is because Medjugorje is in the middle of a Franciscan territory. How sad!

In Medjugorje, I saw the Spirit of God at work: Masses, confessions, prayer, penance, every day, all day long. Can this be wrong, when people are praying, confessing, singing, are happy and being healed spiritually? Certain bishops have not understood that power in the Church does not mean dominating and commanding, but rather service, love and assistance. This is the true meaning of power in the Church, the significance of the episcopate: a bishop must co-ordinate, love, serve and respect the dignity of each person, each priest, be he diocesan or Franciscan.

It seems rather impossible for us to remain deaf to the prophetic grace of Medjugorje. Let us therefore pray for the unity of the local Church where Medjugorje is situated, that it might prepare itself and the whole of the Croatian Church to respond to Our Lady's invitation. In that way, a great obstacle to Gospa's mission will be eliminated. (Echo 136, 3, 74, 2-3).

Daniel Ange's spiritual protest

Daniel Ange

Daniel Ange reacted courageously to the last campaign against Medjugorje, which was launched in good faith in *Famille Chrétienne* following the feast of the Assumption, August 20, 1997, during the chief editor's absence. Daniel was caught in a trap of solidarity, since the two men responsible, while asking for forgiveness in the August 20th edition, could only maintain the magazine's negative stance. A call to the bishop of Mostar's office had confirmed the opposition.

Daniel Ange was at the grand seminary in Prague when he received news of the attack against Medjugorje by the magazine. He immediately wrote to the two people in charge, his friends:

I must tell you how deeply grieved I was by the manner in which you dared write against Medjugorje in the 1022nd edition, and essentially repeating your offence in the

1024th edition on the 28th of August 1997.

He listed the 5 points he disagreed with, and concluded:

I am tempted to advise my bitterly deceived friends to disassociate themselves from you should you persist in this line of conduct.

In that letter, he enclosed his text titled: *"Why bombard the oasis of peace?"* Too extensive to be published in the *Famille Chrétienne*, it was printed in multiple editions, putting many Christians at ease. Daniel Ange said the following:

"I want to speak in the name of a multitude of young people who are painfully grieved, if not scandalized, by your presentation. In the thirty different countries where I have been practising my ministry for more than 20 years, the number of young people who have found or rediscovered God and His Church in Medjugorje is innumerable. Medjugorje is the birthplace of their spiritual life, and their rebirth to life itself."

He based his response (16 pages in the original edition) on spiritual terms. He produced nine authorized documents attesting to the fact that pilgrimages to Medjugorje were neither prohibited nor censured, and that the fundamental question remained open. The judgement of the Church remained suspended. He also responded to the eight most common objections with inspired spiritual clarity. He concluded:

Medjugorje is simply the eternal Gospel proclaimed to the poor of today: a fantastic school of prayer, of formation and evangelization for this generation, the one chosen by God to make the strategic transition from one millennium to the next. I beg you not to shut down this school of divine life and of grace!

Grand Seminary of Prague, Sept. 8-9, 1997

Nativity of the Mother of God and martyrdom of Father Alexandre Men. Signed: Daniel Ange

Famille Chrétienne continued nevertheless on the subject of the apparitions in the first edition of the insert *"Cahiers d'Edifa"* but granted Daniel Ange a four-page interview, which allowed him to summarize his appeal. This is how he defined Medjugorje:

> *A hospital for a wounded generation:*
>
> *How many young people have been delivered from their chains, removed from their prisons, healed of so many physical, psychological and spiritual diseases (among them, Sister Elvira's resurrected drug addicts)! In short, it is the hospice on the road to Jericho, and not only for young people. How many couples are reconciled, families are reunited, and priests (sometimes having abandoned the habit) rediscovering their original fervor. [...] Medjugorje is truly a fantastic school of prayer, of formation and of evangelization: a baptismal school to teach a generation.*
> (Cahiers d'Edifa #1, p. 87-88, 90).

Appreciative of the space accorded him (— there was no question of granting the same to me), Daniel Ange nevertheless felt trapped as a hostage, feeling not only restricted, but placed in a vise between two formidable opponents: J. Bouflet and Bishop Peric. He knew he was not allowed to deal with the fundamental issues.

Shortly after the publishing of the first edition of *Edifa*, he wrote to the editor of *Famille Chrétienne*:

> *I am writing to you as friends, which you truly are. I wish to be truthful with you because I love you. I value your work, and I sympathize with your difficulties. I must express my indignation at the unilateral, and biased manner in which you reported the facts and the interventions by the hierarchy.*
>
> *For the moment, the investigation is not closed. The Ordinary himself declares he is awaiting*

Rome's pronouncement, which has not yet been given. The minimum of objectivity would have called for a simultaneous presentation of the positive factors in favor of the authenticity of Medjugorje along with the negative factors. But you only considered the negative side.

Do not say, "Daniel Ange's interview has sufficiently presented the positive!" You limited me only to the fruit of the apparitions, reserving for yourselves the judgement of the facts and the data on the documents. We were not on the same wavelength.

Thierry Boutet had warned me that you would not print my exact words, because it would be printed elsewhere, and I had agreed. I was stupefied upon discovering the systematic editing of a certain number of interventions dealing with moral issues in the matter and surely through summarizing, the falsification of the contents of other documents.

Here, a note gives precision on the edited documents, notably what was said by the spokesman for the Holy See, Doctor Navarro Valls on the legitimacy of private pilgrimages with pastoral accompaniment. Daniel Ange concluded:

You give the illusion of running an inquiry without ever having gone to Medjugorje, without even consulting those who, for years now, have studied the question at length. Is that right? Is this serious journalism? Honest? Upright?

Do not allow the letter of the law to crush the spirit of the law, or let jurisdiction overcome communion!"

This sentence is of fundamental importance. May it be heard so that it will stop the serious disaffection for the Church. Catholicism is undermined wherever it presents a bureaucratic and autocratic face, closed to the spiritual. Daniel Ange ended his letter with the following:

I ask you to demonstrate fair play and to print this letter. Thank You!

The letter was not published. We are printing it here to show the integrity of our information.

Thanks to Daniel Ange, I can end this accursed chapter with a flourish. In it, the information must dive into the controversy, all the while respecting the sincere opponents, polarized by a conflict which rages, exaggerates the details, strives to destroy reputations in order to destroy Medjugorje and prove that this oasis of grace is nothing but an opportunity for wealth, power and sex! That is how one can summarize the pompous propaganda against Medjugorje today.

Humanly speaking, the adversaries are winning; they have official approval on almost every level. Without equivocation, the Pope has mentioned his attraction for Medjugorje and its fruit. On the other hand, he respects his administration even when it behaves in a manner contrary to his, except for a very serious matter (such as the immediate firing of the director of *Osservatore Romano*, following an article against Lech Valesa). His only detectable intervention in 1997 was the correction of the ambiguous document which seemed to forbid pilgrimages to Medjugorje.

Today those who objectively, peacefully and respectfully defend this place of grace are looked upon as filled with illusions, disobedient or senile, as is murmured in my own case. As I am making this point for the last time, allow me to do so completely and objectively, except for the unspoken reservation that I owe out of respect for the authorities, even when they are in error.

In 1998 as in 1985, it appears Medjugorje will be stifled by the powerful judicial system and the media, skillfully manipulated by the local bishop, who claims he has received no discouragement from the Pope. It remains for us to hope for a supernatural intervention by Our Lady just as it happened in 1986. Our Lady was not able to prevent the condemnation and the death of Her Son, efficiently condemned by the official religious authorities of the day, who were completely convinced they were condemning a fool, a usurper of the truth. Would Gospa and her Son be any happier today? It would be imprudent to presume this.

One must be obedient and respect good order and peace in the Church, even if those in established authority add errors on top of the 105 for which the Pope himself has begged forgiveness during the last 18 years, with his concern for a general confession before the millennium. The silence to which I yield today will make my task much easier. After having rectified so much confusion, error and slander, one at a time (if those actions hit their mark) I will discreetly deposit for safe-keeping the most serious information as Joan of Arc's friends did. Five centuries were necessary to clear her name and recognize her exemplary holiness and heroism.

In her last bulletin, Sister Emmanuel recalled the surprising experience of a parish priest sent on a mission to Medjugorje in 1996 "to gather proof that Mary is not appearing there." He had undertaken his task with zeal. But Mary's presence converted him as it did many others. He returned home saying, "My priesthood was born in Medjugorje."

His bishop was surprised, and his parish in Mexico, where he brings to life the requests of Our Lady, is always full. The church has become too small for the large crowds. It is this grace we wish for the sincere adversaries of Medjugorje, including the first among them, with respect to his convictions (E, June 1st 98).

— Chapter 5 —
FRUITS

The preceding difficult chapters which focussed on the painful details was necessary to see our way through the "bombardments" (Daniel Ange's words), conflicts and complications, where the Prince of Darkness, destroyer and astute twister divider invests the whole of his genius. We have come to the positive and interesting part of the book:

— The basic work (in the present chapter).

— The witnessing: delicious fruit (chapter 6).

Medjugorje continues to grow and bear fruit despite all that is aligned against it to stifle it. The Holy Spirit remains stronger than any human endeavor.

1. THE PARISH

The parish continues its untiring hospitality, more and more difficult to manage as the demands increase. The pre-war numbers of pilgrims have been matched in spite of the warning shots which put the brakes on the progress since the fall of 1997. The co-operation of the parishioners, formed by 17 years of grace and trials, remains a constant resource.

It is a wonder how this rural parish, founded in 1892, can manage so many demanding and contrasting challenges. Catechism and regular local activities would normally keep the parish priests very busy. But they have to oversee the hospitality towards millions of pilgrims, work that is made much more difficult as it is not accepted by the local bishop. It lacks official status and necessary housing, including a church large enough to accommodate the crowds. It lacks the personnel and the mandate. All of these are so important to such a specific and enormous task. The Franciscans are therefore doing their best under enormous strain. They must improvise. They are concerned only with serving the spiritual movement initiated by Our Lady, regardless of the attacks and obstacles. Their response to souls in need is sufficient incentive for them to improvise in a difficult and contested environment. But they calmly go about their work with prayer.

Under these impossible conditions, they manage to give more of themselves to the parishioners during the shorter and shorter quiet times, between January and February.

They do not content themselves with responding. They multiply international spiritual formation meetings. It is the best way for them to prevent any deviation and temptation, which could entrap the work of God and elate so many adversaries who keep a close watch on them. It is an immense undertaking, and requires vigilant attention.

That is why every spring the international leaders gather in Neum from all over the world. This year, 150 leaders from 17 different countries, united in prayer, came to these conclusions:

1. We thank God for giving to his Church [...] new inspiration from the Spirit [...] We are happy that Medjugorje is considered a spiritual movement in the Church of our times.

2. To make our contribution to the renewal of the Church, our duty is to preserve the authenticity of the spiritual movement of Medjugorje, and to offer the testimony of an authentic Christian life based on the messages of Gospa, which express the essence of the Gospel.

3. [...] We have emphasized the need to work for peace in the world, and in the local Church to which the parish of Medjugorje belongs.

The gathering kept away from the quarrels, which opponents like to pick with this oasis of grace.

There are other seminars, begun two years ago, for the formation of pilgrimage guides. Retreats for priests were begun one year ago in early July. Their success produced reservations for this year in greater numbers, and from many more countries.

There are different meetings of young people to cultivate the fruit of pilgrimages, and to maintain in Medjugorje what is too often forgotten elsewhere: the primacy of spirituality.

I also visited *Domus Pacis*, a retreat center established in the parish where fasting and prayer meetings are increasing under the initiative of Raymond Cayrel (4, route du Château Saint-Martin du Bec, BP 14, 76133 Rolleville, tel: 02.35.30.33.75). The retreats last 5 days, from Monday to Friday. The candidates fast on bread and water, including during their sleeper train trip. Slavko is the inexhaustible promoter during these retreats. Members of the Community of the Beatitudes facilitate dialogue for those in need, either for personal conversion, for the deepening of their spiritual growth, or for problems arising from the fasting. The ambiance is extraordinarily wholesome and healthy in spite of the austerity. Young people today are willing to go through a lot, even when the crossbar is placed quite high, as long as the reward is worthwhile.

This colossal task, which I can only sketch, is undertaken in a sort of vise, between two challenges:

— Obedience to the local bishop, who is opposed to the apparitions and anxious to rid them from his parish and the Church.

— Quenching the spiritual thirst of the thousands who descend upon Medjugorje from places where the Spirit is stifled, without nourishment or the possibility of confessions. They find this source of grace in Medjugorje.

The Franciscans are guiding the ship with a steady hand. Last year, one of the best leaders and pilgrimage promoters could have expected high praise for his work, but was rather asked to de-emphasize his self-importance.

Delicate tasks are undertaken in a climate of prayer, trust, dialogue, and humility, without which everything would collapse.

2. PILGRIMS

Following the war, the surge of pilgrimages has continued. The number of communions, which rose from 232,000 to 880,900 between 1992 and 1996, has once again surpassed the one million mark in 1997. The record level of 1,373,850 reached in 1990 and slightly overtaking that of Fatima will probably be surpassed in 1998 despite the efforts to dissuade pilgrimages. This increase is due to the spiritual thirst that Christians from around the world are experiencing. Medjugorje answers a deep need.

The number of Croatian pilgrims has increased along with those from other countries. Some come bare foot as the Portuguese do in Fatima (P, 72, 2; 74, 1).

3. YOUTH FESTIVAL

Founded in 1989, the *Youth Festival* was held in Medjugorje for the eighth time with a record attendance: 8,000 for 1998, 2,000 more than the previous year. The greatest contingent came from eastern block countries (1,200 Czechs, 550 Romanians, 530 Poles, etc.). Medjugorje is a magnet, a source and a fountain of faith for those liberated from communist regimes. All the continents were represented.

This year translation was done in 12 languages (9 the year before), thanks to the improvised use of portable radios. They included French, English, Croatian, Italian, German, Czech, Slovak, Polish, Spanish, Romanian, Korean and Lebanese. The communities of *Les Adoratrices du Precieux Sang*, *Kraljice Mira* of Tomislav Vlasic and an international group of volunteers daily served 1,500 meals for the 8,000 youths. The others managed by themselves.

Joerg Meller, a German psychotherapist who became a priest following his conversion in Medjugorje, opened the festival on Saturday August 2nd. He candidly told of the call he had heard which had led him to give himself totally to God. It gave many the urge to do the same.

At noon Ivan spoke of his experience with prayer. Father Cosimo Cavaluzzo helped those present understand the richness of baptism and to be wary of the pitfalls of the *New Age* movement and other compromised religions of our day:

> *When you young people seek tenderness and love, you have the tendency to throw yourselves into the things of this world, brutalizing yourselves while absorbing like a sponge everything you encounter. When you are seeking tenderness and love, run to Our Lady and throw yourselves into her arms.*

That evening, a long procession wound its way through the streets of Medjugorje, decorated for the occasion.

On Sunday August 3rd, Father Gianni Sgreva, founder of the *Oasis of Peace community* (see p. 117), spoke of Christ and credited Our Lady for a calling he had received during a Mass celebrated in the chapel of apparitions: Give me everything! "Since then I do nothing without her."

On Monday August 4th, Sister Elvira, founder of the *Cenacle* community for the liberation of drug addicts, gave, just as she did the previous year, a measure of her dynamism in a "colorful and peppered" talk as noted by Alexander in *Eco*. She spoke against the vices of the world and of the over-protection of certain Italian families.

Stéphane, a young man preparing for priesthood in the community, revealed the story of Sister Elvira:

> *She waited for 12 years, working in the kitchen of her Congregation before she was able to fulfil her calling and found a community which would service the impossible. "God knows how to accomplish wonderful deeds," said Sister Elvira, singing and dancing on the stage. His resurrection was an explosion of joy [...] If God at times makes us wait, it is because he wants us to mature in love until we draw the whole world to Him.*

Some of the youth from her community gave witness that day, followed by Vicka, Jakov, Mirjana and Jelena. Marija was held up in Italy on the eve of the birth of her third child.

That night, Sister Elvira's Community, once again overflowing with initiative, took charge of the play-bill. For the previous four months, she had been preparing a play centered on the parable of the prodigal son,

Sr. Elvira's rehabilitation center

addressed to the children of the new millennium. First, the descent into hell of a drug addict where, clinging to the very edge of the pit, the Holy Spirit inspires him to cry out: "Abba!" It is at that moment that the Father comes to him. He throws His arms around his neck, kisses him and offers that powerful healing to which we witness so surprisingly in our community, thanks to an evangelistic community life of prayer and work which leads to the Resurrection. The make-shift actors performed with talent and gusto, and had great rapport with the audience.

On Wednesday, August 5th, Fra Jozo Zovko, the parish priest during the summer of 1981 who experienced the apparitions, prison and much more, once again manifested his spiritual radiance and faith. He had had to face many trials and now works for the service of innumerable war orphans of which we will read later.

Alberto Bonifacio, a young bank retiree, totally consecrated to the aid so desperately needed in Bosnia since the beginning of the war, remembered his three companions who were slain on May 29, 1993, in a humanitarian convoy — Fabio, Sergio and Guido. He exemplified Jesus' call: "Whatsoever you do to the least of my children, that you do unto me."

During the closing Mass that evening, the children sang on endlessly in 17 different languages. The Koreans and the Lebanese were the most outstanding.

On the evening of August 6th, as is the tradition, a night of prayer was held on Mount Krizevac from sunset until the dawn of the Feast of the Transfiguration, where the Eucharist was celebrated by Father Slavko and concluded the send-off. All of these youngsters still remain intensely united throughout the world.

The very rich personal exchange of experiences (not theory) reached its peak with the rehabilitated drug addicts of Sister Elvira and the visionaries. They know how to communicate the essence of life and the Christian attitude where they persevere with joy and simplicity.

Father Slavko Barbaric summarized and facilitated the talks with much insight, and promoted a climate of quiet listening and sensitive punctuality that the various situations required. A spirit of unity and dynamic spirituality centered not on the past, but on the future.

The only regret was that the richness of the program did not leave enough time for reflection.

For many that came for the first time, it became a discovery of God and of Mary. The excellent articles written by those young people (Alexander in *Eco* 135 and others) immortalized the spirituality of those days.

4. NEW COMMUNITIES

The two principal communities founded to live the message of Medjugorje continue in depth and simplicity.

The Oasis of Peace

The *Oasis of Peace* continues its rapid development. As I write this, it has 130 members, not counting the associates, that is, those who live in the world either in vowed celibacy or as family members in harmony with wedding vows. Ten centers were established in Italy, and in America  (Brazil and Jamaica). Another is opening in M'Balmayo, Cameroon. The 12 novices of 1997-1998 are completing their formation. Another group is preparing for the fall of 1998.

For Gianni Sgreva, a young Passionist priest, born March 2, 1949 in the diocese of Verona, everything began January 1, 1985. During communion he heard a voice which simply said: "Give yourself totally to me." He recognized this call as coming from Our Lady and immediately responded: *Totus tuus* (Totally yours). Since then, young people are drawn to him in their search for the road to conversion. That is how he came to found the *Oasis of Peace*, to live the message and the grace of Medjugorje in total consecration. On May 25, 1987, the community was constituted in a *Private Association of the Faithful*, by a private judicial agreement. It was canonically recognized as a *Private Association of Faithfuls*, but with a private judicial personality, on December 25, 1990, *ad experimentum* for 5 years, by Monsignor Nicolas Rotunno, Bishop of the suburban diocese Sabina-Poggio Mirteto. Five years later, the new bishop elevated the Community to *Public Association of Faithfuls* with a view to future recognition as an Institute of consecrated life. He approved its charter on December 25, 1996. Two months earlier, on October 19th, the Community had presented the Holy See with an official request for a diocesan recognition as an *Institution of Consecrated Life*.

Fr. Sgreva with Pope John Paul II

It is an amazing group of young people, united and radiant in spite of the austere lifestyle. Eight members trained in the community have already been ordained priests since January 1, 1994. Everything is based on spiritual experiences, characterized by thanksgiving, contemplation, the Eucharist, family spirit, on-going conversion, prayer, fasting, unity and collaboration with Mary, Queen of Peace. The specific goal of the Community is characterized by the vow of peace, which extends from personal life to community life, from the Church, and from Christian unity. They cultivate three charisms: intercession, consecration to the three religious vows, and community life. Each community consists of ten members: brothers and sisters. The number ten was chosen in reference to Genesis 18 where Abraham proposed ten just people to save Sodom and Gomorrah.

The Community rises at 5 a.m., and proceeds in a religious atmosphere without radio or television until night prayers at 9:10 p.m. The essential news of the day, worthy of that word, is read every day in the cafeteria. The adoration of the Blessed Sacrament is perpetual, a brother or sister assuring a continuous presence during the night.

"Kraljice Mira"

The *Kraljice Mira community*, founded by Tomislav Vlasic, continues its development under the responsibility of the Italian Provincial *"ad experimentum"* in accordance with the local bishop. The community presently consists of 63 members in four centers. A dozen other candidates are in waiting.

Within this community, Tomislav Vlasic's preaching has caused 100 fraternities to be born, living the same spirituality in the world in groups of consecrated laity. Others follow the same path individually, living the same spirit of oblation. During 1997, Tomislav Vlasic held four great three-day meetings throughout Italy with a participation of between 400 and 800 candidates. Other one-day meetings (one of which attracted 3,000 persons) were held on Don Bosco hill. Other meetings are held during the afternoon in various sanctuaries. Tomislav Vlasic has faith in the dynamism of the Holy Spirit Who is affirming Himself as we near the millennium. He does so without ignoring the reprisals which never fail to oppose the great manifestations of the Holy Spirit.

Queen of Peace Community

Birmingham, Alabama

Terry Colafrancesco, 43 year old ex-landscaper and father of 7, established a sort of American Medjugorje II, outside of Birmingham, Alabama (USA) where a community of 50 people resides, families with numerous children. They attend school in the community but not college, as they learn more healthy manual skills. The community leads a simple fervent lifestyle, printing books and magazines. Their neighbors have recourse to the workshops they have founded in the community. They live as a self-sufficient group, with the help of a few donations. Marija, who visited the community on many occasions, transmitted this message from Our Lady:

— "I want you to be the joy of life."

They have also received personal messages.[1]

I have no news from the other communities mentioned in previous volumes, but most are still active.

If people in authority bring about a negative judgement on Medjugorje, what would become of the vocations born of Medjugorje?

If we plan on purifying the Church by this negative route, can we see the risks of such a spiritual abortion?

5. PRAYER GROUPS

On July 15, 1997, Ivan celebrated the 15th anniversary of his prayer group. They meet twice a week — Tuesday on the hill of apparitions and Friday on Mount Krizevac, with or without Ivan's presence. When he is present, there is an apparition.

Jelena's group, dispersed at the end of her adolescence because of the studies, marriage and employment of each young girl, started up again after Jelena's return in 1997. This demonstrated the vitality of prayer, which has lasted.

Medjugorje has led to the formation of thousands of prayer groups the world over, especially in America, Austria and Italy. Their dynamism seems equal to the prayer groups of the Charismatic Renewal, another great phenomenon in the world today.

That Renewal is recognized for what it truly is. Why then is Medjugorje so little recognized, so severely contested?

6. CONFERENCES AND GATHERINGS

Medjugorje continues to inspire a large number of conferences and gatherings, especially in the USA.

On October 22nd, in Washington DC, Chris Smith, a congressman involved with Action for Peace, and president of *Congressional Human Rights Caucus*, invited Sister Emmanuel to speak to 200 members of his group on the message of Medjugorje where he sees a basis for the cause of peace in Bosnia-Herzegovina. The invitation came following a television program produced in 1997. It was broadcast every week in 1998 on an American network. Sister Emmanuel spoke for an hour and Chris Smith asked her to lead the group in prayer for the *promotion of human rights throughout the world, through Our Lady, visitor of Medjugorje.* Five or six congressmen were present at that meeting. One of the organizers was so happy he could not get to sleep that night and went down to the chapel to pray in thanksgiving. The weekly program, which had provided that invitation, was called: *"Medjugorje, our Mother's Final Call."*

When Sister Emmanuel went to retrieve her passport, she was told that M. Tudjman, President of the

Croatian Republic, wished to give it to her personally. It was part of a ceremony of thanksgiving for her actions during the war when she and two other members of her community were the only remaining non-Croats in the village.

Sr. Emmanuel

Following this recognition, Sister Emmanuel was invited to the eighth *Medjugorje Peace* conference, October 24-26. On August 28th, Sister Emmanuel was warned by the organizer that the sanctuary of the *Queen of Peace* preferred that she abstain at the request of the parish of Medjugorje, no doubt sensitive to "propaganda" levelled against it. And yet the invitation had been a spontaneous one. Father Slavko explained to Sister Emmanuel that he himself had at times been asked to refrain from attending such events for reasons of political correctness. There was no doctrinal criticism against her. The matter concerned small internal problems, her radiance at times overshadowing certain competent organizations. The issue should not be pursued.

However, the credit given to Sister Emmanuel in the USA caused her to be accused by the fundamentalist press. *The Wanderer* characterized her as fraudulent. She was in good company since Bishop Hnilica, Confessor of the faith during the Marxist persecution, a friend of the Pope and founder of a flourishing community with a high level of spirituality, was called a "criminal" by that same newsprint.

Bishop Nicholas d'Antonio (81 years old) decided to help Sister Emmanuel. On August 28, he wrote:

Dear Sister Emmanuel,

I was literally heart-broken when I heard of the terrible slander [...] Jesus and Mary also had to suffer. Remember the words of the Gospel of John 16, 33: "Here on earth you will have many trials and sorrows; but take courage, for I have overcome the world." (Letter of August 28, 1997).

On March 9th, the same bishop supported the cause of Sister Emmanuel so that her news reports continued to be distributed in the USA.

We have mentioned the eighth Spanish congress held in Medjugorje on August 25, 1997.

Another congress, organized by Father O'Connor and Brian Miller, was held at the University of Notre Dame on the feast of Pentecost, 1998. I was invited but could not attend because of previous obligations in Birmingham.

7. ECHOS, RADIOS, CASSETTES

Among the numerous publications on Medjugorje, the first in importance is *Echo of Medjugorje*, originating in Italy, translated into 11 languages, and with a total circulation nearing one million.

The parish of Medjugorje prints its news bulletin *Glas Mira* (in Croatian), and its bi-monthly *Press Bulletin* is spread throughout the world by fax and Internet. In obedience to the bishop, they do not print the messages.

The various newsletters and bulletins are listed on p. 13-14. I thank them once again for their contribution.

Vicka speaking on Radio Maria in the presence of director Fr. Livio and Alvaro.

The radio stations inspired by the Medjugorje groups continue. In Poland, *Radio Maria* is such a success and has such a strong influence that it was credited with swaying the Polish vote against abortion in spite of its being legalized by the communist regime many years ago. There again, an excessive success can be frightening. Cardinal Glemp intervened to invite this radio station to a more modest influence.

It would be too tiresome to try and list all the audio and videotapes published for the purpose of spiritual formation.

Answering machines continue also and the Internet is filled with information on Medjugorje. As for writings, the increase seems limitless and it is an invitation for me to retire after this 17th volume of *Latest News*.

8. HEALINGS

The news reports on healings are subdued. Sister Emmanuel, who encountered many rarely speaks of them anymore, perhaps having been invited to be prudent. Back from the USA, she related the following testimony from a young couple:

A baby is saved

Cherry and Ron dreamed of having a child. Finally, after eight long years, their dream was fulfilled. Their joy was at its highest when they went for the first ultrasound. The image was excellent but the baby was not moving, as it should at that stage of development. The second ultrasound revealed an irreversible heart disease which could only lead to the baby's death. The future parents' grief was intense. They immediately began praying fervently while friends and relatives suggested they abort the child and not wait for death to come. Cherry and Ron could not accept the fact that they were about to lose this little life which they already loved so much. The child must be operated on despite the odds. The doctors attempted a blood transfusion in the umbilical cord because the child was terribly anemic. The pregnancy was only 23 weeks old and death was imminent. Following that physically and morally challenging operation, Cherry and Ron returned home, heart-broken.

Cherry remembered a wooden rosary her friend Lise had brought back from Medjugorje and which she had buried in a drawer with other useless articles. She was inspired to place the rosary on her stomach as she prayed in order for her child to feel it. She will never forget that moment. For the very first time, she felt the child kick. It felt like her daughter was trying to grasp the rosary. Over the next few days, every time Cherry and Ron sat down to pray the rosary, the little one would manifest its presence in her mother's womb.

Cherry asked for a new ultrasound. Ron prayed near the apparatus, when suddenly the doctor called all the medical personnel to come and see the screen: all the excess water, which had gorged the body of the child and was about to cause its death, had completely disappeared. The doctors could not get over it. There was no explanation. They asked the couple to go home and allow the baby to be born normally. There was no need for an operation.

Anna-Mary was born in September, 1994. I saw her last month (May) in the USA. She is healthy and joyful. She runs around every-where. Her parents have become apostles for Mary. They invite their relatives and friends to pray the rosary, for it is the source of miracles. They hope to go to Medjugorje in thanksgiving (Echo, June 15, 1997).

This is not meant to attribute magical powers to the rosary, or to pretend that such healings are systematic. God sometimes permits proof. Through prayer the Cross also becomes a source of joy, as Gospa says. Many healings are not granted for lack of prayer and fasting for the sick. Our Lady of the Miraculous Medal told Catherine Labouré (1830): "There are graces that remain in waiting for lack of prayer."

A fruitful benediction

During a conference in Medjugorje, Nicole related her brother Xavier's healing and conversion.

On February 24, 1997, Xavier went to Paris for a chest scan to verify a diagnosis he had been given of lung cancer. When the time for the test came, the apparatus broke down. We decided to go for a bite to eat while repairs were being done to the scanner. I didn't know what to say during the meal. Having just returned from Medjugorje, I followed Mary's advice and silently, mentally blessed my brother with the blessing Our Lady uses. He felt something and asked:

— "What are you doing?"

I answered sheepishly because he wasn't very open to this kind of thing.

— "Why are you asking me that question?"

— "I don't know why but I'm asking it again."

— "I blessed you with Mary's blessing."

— "And what does that blessing do?"

— "It heals and brings conversion."

— "Ah no! That would be too easy; a swipe with a sponge and everything's okay."

He nevertheless took a clipping from the L'Etoile newsprint on Medjugorje. And he saw the light.

That evening, at supper, he told me:

— "I went to confession this afternoon at 5:30 p.m. I felt an urge to go."

The confession had lasted a profound 30 minutes, and had not been without tears. His life changed radically just at the time of the apparition. Today he speaks openly of it to his friends and clients, and goes to Mass every day. He has found peace. His faith is deepening and he has traveled many times to Medjugorje.

He was operated on March 18th following the diagnosis: "cancerous cells on trans-thoracic biopsy." However, analysis on the operated section was: "pulmonary tumor, benign, non-cancerous." The difference has not been explained.

Get up and walk

Alberto Bonifacio witnesses:

On March 17, 1998 during Mass, I noticed a young man in a wheel chair. All of a sudden he began to scream incomprehensibly. He was taken out of the sanctuary because his cries were a disturbance.

The next day, March 18th, he was present for Mirjana's apparition, and I had the opportunity of speaking with him. He is Italian. His name is Andrea and he is 15 years old.

The previous evening, Mass had hardly begun when Andrea began to scream. His father had taken him from his wheel chair and placed him on a bench. Still shouting at the top of his lungs, he began to take a few steps, his first. His father was standing behind him, ready to catch him should he fall. Fra Svetozar Kraljevic asked them to leave as the shouting was disturbing the celebration. Andrea, still shouting turned and walked out of the church. He walked all the way down the center aisle, which was left open for security reasons. What was he shouting? His parents translated:

— "The Lord is telling me to walk."

Some friends from our group arrived at the church after Mass sometime around 7 p.m. and saw Andrea sitting in his wheel chair surrounded by his parents and other friends in front of the sanctuary. The group was bustling about. Someone asked Andrea to get up and walk. He got up and began walking, speaking also with a clear voice.

— "The Lord is telling me to walk."

His hands and face muscles were now normal and not contracted as before. Someone stood in front of him to help him control his still uncertain steps, similar to those of a one-year old infant. He crossed the space in front of the sanctuary from right to left, and tried a few steps. His mother and father were in tears. Our friend Nori asked the mother:

— "Has he never walked?"

— "No, Miss, he began walking in the church. It was embarrassing because we couldn't understand what he was shouting. That was why we came out."

Andrea was also in tears. He began to realize how his life was changing. A superior level of love overwhelmed him. He finally left for his hotel with his parents while the pilgrims who surrounded them glorified God. To glorify God for such graces is unfortunately frowned upon these days.

I am not called to prejudge how valuable such a spectacular healing is, but it will not be examined but buried, like the bleeding Host which had impressed an American presbytery but which was ordered hushed up by the local bishop. God is forbidden from performing miracles in that place. (I abridged and concluded Bonaficio's story, April 1998).

Physical and spiritual improvement

Bernadette Weber, whom I have met many times at Roc Estello, is thankful for physical as well as spiritual improvements. She is hoping for a complete healing. Here is an edited version of her witnessing:

From the onset of the disease which hit me in 1990, I accepted, and prayed, with neither anger nor rebelliousness. These physical difficulties have helped me journey spiritually. In November 1990, during the feast of All Saints, I was incapacitated by a sciatic nerve problem. This worsened from week to week.

In December, a myelo-graphic examination discovered a herniated disc, which was finally operated on the 24th of January, 1991 in Rheims. I had some difficulty resuming my work as a teacher in May 1991. On June 1st, I came to a complete stop, unable to move at all. I was transported by ambulance to a rheumatologist in Rheims. When school opened for the fall semester, I was unable to return to work, due to pain.

December 1991: the neurosurgeon who operated on me discovered crippling, incurable after-effects, affecting my ability to walk.

September 1992: New examination by Professor Rey at the Beaujon hospital in Clichy. Same pessimistic diagnosis, new tests (MRI). The diagnosis still didn't offer any solution, but I didn't give up hope.

April 1993: I made a pilgrimage to Medjugorje. The car trip was long and painful. On arrival, and to the amazement of other pilgrims, I proceeded to climb Mount Krizevac without even considering the sharp rocks on the path.

— "Look, she seems to be flying," a priest said to his group.

I came down just as easily. Having started back after the other members of the group, I quickly caught up to them at the third station and continued down at the same speed.

The next day, I was in pain again. When I got home, my eyes were bright and my skin tone was normal.

Before departing for Medjugorje, I took six pills a day: three Myolastan and three Di-Antalvic. When I came home, none at all. I returned to teaching. I still had pain but something had changed.

From December 1995 to October 1996, I suffered a relapse following a fall in class in which I tried to avoid a couple of students. I was suffering once again from a pinched sciatic nerve: this time on the right side.

In April 1996, I was off work for a month, following a pilgrimage to San Giovanni Rotondo at Padre Pio's. But the improvement continued and I could move about with more and more ease. Today I can stand up by myself but not for very long. I now live an almost normal existence. My spiritual progress is continuing, in peace, with a renewed love of prayer and an inner desire to help those who have difficulties like mine. I can't help but hope for a complete healing.

This case may not be significant from a physical point of view, but I report it for its spiritual progress and hope.

What interests me in this case is that the hope for a complete healing sustains a true spiritual growth with gratifying improvements along the way. There is not enough evidence for a full investigation but it deserves more than a negative hatchet job. Jesus did not condemn but rather encouraged those who hoped in Him for a healing. He repeats throughout the Gospel:

— "Your faith has saved you."

— "I have never seen such faith in Israel."

In both instances, there is no question of faith in miracles which today is so severely frowned upon.

Debra and John Dinolfo's research

I first interacted with Debra and John Dinolfo in the USA during the summer of 1997. The have undertaken a study of some of the many healings happening throughout North America. They are preparing a book, based on thorough study and supported by medical documentation. We are eagerly awaiting its publication. Here are a few of the healings I had not heard about and which are compiled in their research.

Miriam Bergeron (Rhode Island)

Miriam Bergeron (in her early forties) suffered a traumatic fall down a flight of stairs on September 25, 1990. The brain was damaged. She was unable to speak coherently and could not recognize her husband. She left the hospital in December, 1990 with crippling effects, suffering daily epileptic seizures and unable to take tranquilizers because of allergies. At home she was cared for by her husband Victor, an air conditioning technician and their six children aged from 15 to 28, most of them still at home.

Victor first heard of Medjugorje in the summer of 1991. Although he was not very religious at the time, he decided to take his wife there and hope for a cure. The trip was not easy as it took place during the war. Upon arriving at Washington National Airport Victor discovered their booking on a flight to Sarajevo had been cancelled. He firmly insisted on the next flight to

Sarajevo, the sad capital of Bosnia in dire straights; the couple finally arrived in Sarajevo and from there flew to Mostar. It took two days to get to Medjugorje.

On August 11th, the Bergerons attended a healing mass in Tihaljina, celebrated by Father Jozo Zovko. Both experienced resting in the Spirit.[2] The husband got up first. Father Jozo invited Miriam to remain as she was until she felt the urge to get up. About fifteen minutes later she got up. On her return to the hospital she was surprised to be able to read and to converse normally. When the couple returned to Rhode Island, everyone was amazed at Miriam's reading (which she could not do before), her normal speech and her overall health.[3] Today she remains healthy and participates with her husband in a prayer group in Riverside, Rhode Island and in humanitarian aid services.

Miriam's health is not perfect. She still suffers from lupus, as she did before her fall, but all the major neurological handicaps resulting from her accident were healed during her pilgrimage to Medjugorje, on August 12, 1991.

Debra and John Dinolfo are gathering the medical files on this healing. A neurologist was consulted. The diagnosis, after the traumatic accident in 1990 following clinical assessments and magnetic resonance imaging, was "bifrontal brain contusions with cerebral hemorrhage and endema."

Virginia Rose (Rhode Island)

In 1986 Virginia Rose, a 41-year-old mother of two, was struck by a relentless disease, which eventually reduced her muscle tone until she was condemned to a wheel chair. A Harvard neurologist diagnosed multiple sclerosis. Virginia prayed the rosary regularly upon the advice of a physical therapist who recently had returned from Medjugorje.

In June 1991 she left for Bosnia, via Rome. During a prayer meeting, Father Peter Mary Rookey invited her to stand up from her wheelchair. She did so and walked to St. James church to give thanks to God and then to the Hill of Apparitions. John and Debra Dinolfo continue gathering medical records on this healing.

Marie Siriani (Connecticut)

Marie Siriani of Shelton Connecticut was born June 23, 1941. In March of 1989 she underwent a single radical masectomy to try to stop the spread of breast cancer. At that point her prognosis was poor, according to her oncologist Dr. Kenneth Sacks.

In Medjugorje, on October 4, 1989, feast of Saint Francis of Assisi, Marie and her husband Carl prayed with Vicka. Mrs. Siriani felt a sudden heat penetrate throughout her body. She was immediately convinced of a healing.

Two months after the couple returned to the USA, Marie ceased receiving chemotherapy, but upon her doctor's request she continued taking the anti-cancer drug, Tamoxifen, until 1994.

Mrs. Siriani remains in excellent health, according to Dr. Sacks. He believes her recovery is extraordinary. He has always been impressed by Marie Siriani's strength of soul, rooted in a faith she openly professes.

The Dinolfos continue their inquiry from which these accounts of healing were gleaned. The information and documents they need regarding some healings are not easy to obtain.

Rita Klaus' amazing healing (DN 10, 37-38; 13, 85) was published in the autobiography of her life. (In English, Orleans, Massachusetts, 1993 and in Italian, 1997).

9. SOCIAL DIMENSION

Medjugorje has been labeled as "sentimental piety." The war in Bosnia has revealed a humanitarian dimension to many pilgrims confronted by the immense needs, not only in Medjugorje but in all of Herzegovina, Orthodox and Muslims included. The pilgrims of Medjugorje have large and generous hearts.

Medjugorje for children

The Swiss pianist, Mauro Hasch, born in Lugano, founded the first humanitarian aid center to help the children of Latin America and then those of Medjugorje. On the tenth anniversary of its foundation, he spoke about the origin of this initiative:

> *I was at the time a tepid Christian and defiant towards the Church...through transcendental meditation and Raja Yoga, I had learned how to exercise a positive influence on my inner concentration. This did not lead me to a true enjoyment of life. One day, thumbing through a magazine, I came across an article on Medjugorje. That was in August of 1984. From that moment on, I felt an urge to go. I also had a dream where I saw a splendid rainbow (...) In November 1984, I made up my mind and went to Medjugorje on February 19, 1985.*

His deepening faith led him to these concrete decisions:

> *Very quickly I realized that faith needs to be made concrete by charitable works. Day after day there grew in me a desire to help those who suffer, especially children who risk death in third world countries. I got in touch with humanitarian organizations, but their political*

orientations did not convince me. It was in Medjugorje that I found the spirit of fraternity and unity on a world level, and with cultural diversity. I decided to establish a humanitarian organization that transcended all political or ideological particularity, and that acted directly, without intermediary, in a spirit of true fraternity. That was how, on December 31, 1987, "Medjugorje for Children" was born, officially recognized in March, 1988 by the Swiss confederation.

That was how, in Brazil and in India, villages were set up to receive abandoned children. In Brazil homeless children roam the big cities like wild animals and the police shoot at them when they steal.

The foundation was established in Medjugorje since the onset of the war. It has helped with the construction of the *"Village de la Mère"*, founded by Slavko for children and widows. The first house sheltered seven children, Sister Zdenka Kozina and Mrs. Rusic, exiled from Konjic. Mrs. Rusic is the mother of a Herzegovina Franciscan, Father Dragan Rusic.

To amplify his international works, Mauro Harsch organized a chamber music concert in Lugano on the tenth anniversary, under the direction of Carlo Maria Giulini. The benefits of the concert were used to finance the studies of young Bosnians from age 16 to 22 and to supply food and medicine during the war. He also recorded a CD of Mozart and Chopin at the same benefit.

The association prints a quarterly: *Germogli* (the buds), to spread to children about the spirit and service of Mary. *Germogli* is a beautiful magazine illustrated with children's photos. Children are interviewed, news bulletins from other centers are published, and lists of appeals come from Madagascar and Romania, etc. (No. 6, Summer 1997).

Sister Elvira

We spoke of Sister Elvira's rehabilitated drug-addicts earlier during the youth festival (p. 113). They are also permanent witnesses for pilgrims. We remain in awe of their prayer life and their hard work to which they openly witness, in stark contrast to the usual fatality. They show no trace of the past, which generally scars the psyche or the body itself. It is one of the miracles of Medjugorje and of Sister Elvira who is opening other such homes throughout the world. Vicka, the ardent sponsor of the homes, is always present for the youngsters who are organized in perfect self-management.

Sr. Elvira (right) with the Pope.

An orphans' village in Jakljan

Father Jozo Zovko built his village for children on an island in the Adriatic: Jakljan. The photos show healthy children living peacefully on the shores of the Adriatic. Their parents were slain during the war. Life is reborn in a healthy body and mind under the protection of Our Lady's mantle.

Dana Filipovic, taken in by Fra Jozo, shares her thanksgiving:

August 19, 1992 was very hard for me when I lost my father whom I loved so much. I could not believe that I didn't have him anymore and to this day I still can't believe it (written in

Children who have lost one or both parents in the war.

1996). Mother, who prays to God every day, used to get up at 6 a.m. to go to work and come home at 5:30 p.m. When she smiles, she has a little dimple in her chin.

When I arrived on the island, I could not imagine having to pray a full rosary, and yet I saw the joy and peace in the mothers and children through that prayer. I started to sense that God is with us. He has reunited us and is protecting us. I discovered the importance of God in our lives. I found the union of hearts as in a united family. I started to love Jesus more and more every day, and being attracted to daily morning Mass and the rosary during the evening. This place has awakened in me a desire for God. [...]

I've always desired to love and be loved. Now I have found God! He loves me and I love Him. Now I know that the greatest love is the love that comes from God. I would like to ask everyone to pray, and by that prayer to realize a righteous life that will lead to God. We are not alone. He is always with us. [...] We also have a Mother who never abandons us, the Blessed Virgin Mary. (*Medjunarodno Kumstvo Djetedu*, is the name of the publication edited by this movement of the Father for the orphans of Father Jozo: *Mir I dobro*, 1997, Varese, Italy, telephone fax: +39 332487813).

The island of Jakljan was given to Father Jozo's foundation by the Croatian government which has had 2,800 children adopted through sponsorship. *Mir I Dobro* has helped Fra Jozo realize the complete restoration of a four-story building and 26 bungalows, abandoned after the war — many roofs to repair!

Father Jozo continues his spiritual travels to mobilize the world's attention and efforts to relieve the wounds and sufferings created by the war in Bosnia. He invites all to help. The assistance provided by the association is immense. Since December 1991, 48 villages of Bosnia

Holy Family Institute under construction in Siroki Brijeg. Home for orphaned children. Pictured above (left): George and Angela Ivanich - Canadian representatives for Fr. Jozo's Godparent Program.

have received help which is distributed to all people, regardless of their race or creed. Father Jozo's monastery in Siroki Brijeg has opened a large distribution center for clothing, food and medication for the people of Bosnia-Herzegovina.

A center was opened in the monastery for Croatian and Muslim refugees fleeing Bosnia — hundreds of women and children. A radio station began transmitting in 1994 to help mobilize urgent needs. The sick are transported to Italy for operations and prosthesis.

Father Orec, a Franciscan and ex-parish priest of Medjugorje, also deprived of canonical mission in the Mostar diocese, has founded a large humanitarian aid center in Spilt. He provides countless prosthesis for the victims of the war. Appointed recently to the Mother House in Rome, he remains in touch with this efficient enterprise and visits one week out of every month.

Other humanitarian aid

Help for the needy continues, notably in the organizations founded on site (already listed in DN 16, p. 77) and the following:

— *Medjugorje Mir* association,

— *Medjunarodno Kumstvo Djetedu Herzeg-Bosnia*, founded in 1992 at Siroki Brijeg by Fra Jozo Zovko to help 3,400 sponsored children, and assist the families of the wounded,

— *Medjugorje Djeci Poginulih Branitelja* fund, started by Slavko Barbaric to support orphans,

— *Prijatelji Talenata* fund, also started by Slavko to support students,

— *Majcino Selo: Mothers' Village*, in full development in Medjugorje for widows and orphans,

— Father Svetozar Kraljevic's organization to mobilize aid from English speaking countries.

— Chapter 6 —

TESTIMONIES

Each day of Medjugorje is filled with great and small events which sometimes change lives, bringing souls closer to Our Lord and Our Lady. Many will give thanks for the rest of their lives.

Let us continue, as we do every year, with this comforting chapter of spiritual goodness, patronage and small flowers. They do not have the heroic color as the stories during the war, but are a testimony to the vigilance and maternal power of Our Lady. Every year we could fill a book ten times as large as this one. We chose a few, not for their importance but to give a hint of the variety of graces — a few flowers from a vast prairie.

1. INTERIOR HEALINGS

Reconciliation

A woman in distress went to see Marija:

— "I came to you because I don't have the courage to go to a priest. I don't dare go to confession. I've had eight abortions and I'm afraid the priest will get angry and throw me out of the confessional. But you, you can do something: ask Our Lady to help me. I can't sleep anymore; I'm completely depressed, I ache all over and I suffer terribly. My husband is totally opposed to life. We do not have much income. Now I can't have any more children. Can you confide all of this to Gospa?

Marija, who was expecting her third child at the time, confided this distressing situation to Gospa that very night. She received the following answer:

— *From now on, she will be the bearer of life for those in need.*

That woman reconciled herself to God, went to confession and was so transformed that she now witnesses daily with great healing power. She tells women who are considering abortion about her bitter experience in order to dissuade them from going through with it. She also visits hospitals.

By so doing, she has convinced one woman to keep the child she was carrying (M, May 1997, #38, p. 56).

Mary's victory on drugs

On an island in the Indian Ocean, a father had worked very hard to send his son to school in London. Everything went well for the first two years. But during his third year, the temptation of drugs got the best of him. He wrote to his father that he had abandoned his studies and was now roaming the streets aimlessly. His father shed every tear in his body. He feared the worst. Why had he made all those sacrifices? His wife and he were fervent Christians and knew of the message of Medjugorje. They decided to have total faith in Mary to save their son. The father was inspired to make a very difficult sacrifice. He quit smoking although he had been smoking two packs a day. He stood firm for love of his son.

A short while later he received an enthusiastic letter:

— "Father, I've returned to university. It's a real miracle! One day, without my doing anything particular, I got this great distaste for drugs. I stopped and pondered, and I felt an interior force, which was urging me to continue with my classes."

That deliverance took place shortly after his father had quit smoking. He related this story to Sister Emmanuel, crying with joy.

Faith obtains everything! (E 1, 8. 1997).

2. GRACES AND CONVERSIONS

Letter to Our Lady

At a social gathering, Lucie spoke of her next pilgrimage to Medjugorje:

She could take letters of petition for Mary, which she would hand over to Vicka who would place them at Gospa's feet.

An atheistic neighbor (communist) heard of this and as he had serious family problems, handed Lucie a letter expressing his intentions, for Gospa (just in case!).

— "Ah! If that woman could do something!"

— "I will pray for you, but in turn, you must also recite an Our Father and a Hail Mary with your wife each of the seven days of my pilgrimage."

He didn't know the prayers but found written copies.

Upon her return, Lucie got a visit from that same neighbor:

— "I came to thank you because my daughter, who hadn't worked in over two years, received two job offers during those seven days. We are so happy for her! She is mighty powerful, that Gospa! He doesn't say 'that woman' anymore."

Five months later, Lucie met the neighbor's wife who told her:

— "Those prayers you recommended to my husband, we can't do without them. We recite them every day."

Yes, in Medjugorje, those messages described as "dumb" become fruitful in the hearts of the pilgrims (E).

New outlook

I received this letter on November 27, 1997 (CR, Cabourg):

I was converted in a radical and spectacular fashion in Medjugorje on November 1, 1996. The moment of outpouring of the Holy Spirit was a moment of great power, which has radically changed the reason for my existence.

Before this conversion, I was far from God. I believed, but my faith was so small...

I needed to believe, but I didn't fully realize that Our Lady, God, Jesus and the Holy Spirit *existed*, that they were truly alive, active and energetic! It was unthinkable for me, even inconceivable. The day of that outpouring, I thought that heaven was going to fall on my head. On my return from Bosnia, I was bedridden for eight days, repeating to myself non-stop: "How could I have been hit so hard? How?"

That 'saving' moment had been accompanied by a review of my life. Along with that radical outpouring, Our Lady and the Holy Spirit asked me to act and to create for them. That is why I am writing. (The rest concerns personal projects, hence my discretion).

I hope Father Jozo — he who saw in me and before me, a great grace I was about to live — will be the sponsor of what Our Lady asked of me. It is a pious vow, but with Our Lady, you never know!

I realize my extreme good fortune in experiencing such moments, powerful and unmistakeable, but I especially realize the great privilege Our Lady gave me, suggesting from Heaven my mission on earth. She is a great and Holy Lady, this Virgin Mary, gentle but determined.

[...] How do I express what they told me, without deceiving myself? [...]

I received, during another visit to Medjugorje, a great grace that gave me the courage to witness.

3. VOCATIONS AND PRIESTHOOD

Spiritual healing

In August, 1988, John Sweeney, a brilliant 25-year-old manager in Manhattan, had decided he would be a millionaire before age 30. His rate of success encouraged him to believe he would attain that goal before the set date.

At that time, he doubted God's existence and his lifestyle reflected that doubt. Nevertheless, out of curiosity, he decided to travel to Medjugorje with his pious sister and a business associate who had spoken to him of this place.

On August 6, 1988, the feast of the Transfiguration, the trio left for Dubrovnik. They arrived in Medjugorje by car on the 8th of August. During a prayer meeting on the Hill of Apparitions, John had a direct and extraordinary experience of God the Father's love through the intercession of the Virgin Mary. It occurred during Ivan's apparition, around 11 p.m. John was quite near

Ivan and looked at his rapture with an intense interest which was sharpened by the twilight. Over the next few days, a transformation began to take place in him, a spirit of repentance and of the joy arising from the depth of his being.

Back home in New York, he was a different man. He invited his clients and friends for breakfast to speak of Our Lady and of her messages of peace and conversion. A few months later, he abandoned his promising career.

He came back to Medjugorje during the summer of 1989, moved into a home for pilgrims, and spoke with Father Slavko Barbaric, Milona von Hapsburg and many others. He then left to spend a few months in Fatima where he discerned a vocation to the priesthood.

In 1990 he joined the Franciscan order in Zagreb. In 1991 he met the Pope in Rome, then completed his studies and formation in different Franciscan houses in the USA. He branched off from the Franciscans OFM (Order of Friars Minor) to the new religious family called Franciscans of the Primitive Observance, which he founded with many companions under the authority of Monsignor Sean O'Malley, Capuchin monk and Bishop of Fall River, Massachusetts. He now resides in the New Bedford monastery where he was ordained priest on December 19, 1998. The New Order is consecrated to the service of youth, following directives of a message from Medjugorje. He is already preaching retreats where he manifests a special charism for teaching teenagers, including those who are hooked on drugs, alcohol and other dependencies.

Some satisfied priests

In July 1997, after the first retreat for priests in Medjugorje, one of them (35 years old) told Sister Emmanuel:

— "I had never seen anything like that. In all the retreats I've been to, they had us working with our heads. Here, it's the heart. Our Lady is cleaning up my house, shaking carpets and moving the furniture. Everything is being displaced. I count on her to rearrange everything."

A Polish priest had this to say:

— "I've received the grace of not being afraid to speak to others. A great peace entered me, invading my whole being. I'm going to come back with my family and colleagues."

A parish priest:

— "I knew with my head that prayer is important, but here I've experienced it as the foundation of my life. I've decided to commit a lot of time to prayer. As for fasting, I'm going to start with one day a week."

None of the priests left Medjugorje unchanged (E).

A renewed priesthood

Joseph Quinn was a 9-year-old Dutch boy. His uncle, suffering from cancer, was preparing for a pilgrimage to Lourdes. He was amazed to see friends and neighbors giving his uncle mysterious envelopes.

— "They are petitions entrusted to Our Lady of Lourdes," his mother told him. "She will grant them."

An idea germinated in the boy's head. He ran to his room and did his best to write:

— "Dear Mary, make me a priest! Your son, Joseph."

At that time he recited the rosary with his family without thinking about it too much. He accepted, but his heart was not in it. He knew from his mother that Mary was marvelous. Our Lady took him at his word. He was ordained in 1995.

On October 5, 1997, in Medjugorje, he celebrated Mass, expressing his happiness at being a priest, bringing the anglophone priests sitting near him to tears.

— "For me, changing the bread and wine into the Body and Blood of Christ is always an overwhelming experience. Even so, after this pilgrimage to Medjugorje, I realize that I am only now becoming a real priest. I've discovered here the depth of prayer. I would like to tell all priests and bishops:

— "Come! Come! Come to learn to pray, pray, pray." (E, October 15,1997).

4. LITTLE FLOWERS

"Jesus, I give you my fear"

Clotilde (Beatitudes) relates:

On Good Friday, coming down Mount Krizevac, following the Way of the Cross, Christiane and I served as Guardian Angels to Aude, a young physically handicapped psychomoter. Aude was having an anxiety attack looking down at the steep slope. Seeing her rigid with spasms, Christiane stopped to catch her breath and tried to calm her. She asked Aude to repeat: "Jesus, I place my trust in you." Aude repeated the words, timidly at first, then with more and more confidence. Christiane had her repeat: "Jesus, I give you my fear." Aude repeated this three times before being able to say the phrase with conviction. Then Christiane told her: "We can continue. Your fear is gone because you've given it to Jesus."

All along the descent, as soon as an obstacle appeared, Aude would say: "Jesus, I trust in you!" and she would then overcome each obstacle with a sure step. Once, she was thrown off balance but said again: "Jesus, I trust in you." When we arrived at the first station of the Cross at the bottom of the hill, where Jesus is condemned to death, Aude told us: "I am like Jesus! People mock me but I can't say anything; I pray." In her childish joy, she saw as a gift the fact of being the first of her group to arrive at the bottom of the hill (E, April 15).

Apparition

This pilgrim came from the east where he had been managing a small store for the last 7 years. Having come to Medjugorje, he prayed in front of Our Lady's statue on the right side of the church. He saw Our Lady herself in that statue, real, alive, and incredibly beautiful. She did not say anything, but, filled with joy and gratitude, she looked at every person who approached her to pray. She accepts all prayer with wonder, and accompanies those who leave with a look of tenderness. He told Sister Emmanuel:

— "She looked at me with so much joy that I was overwhelmed. It seemed as if, for her, I was the most important person in the world. I remained there for a long time, looking at her and praying. When my prayers were over, she was still there. I left telling myself that tomorrow she would still be there. But when I came back with my wife, she was gone.

"I've never again seen her as on that day, but a fire of love has been burning in my heart. When I meet someone, I see Jesus in that person, as if it is Jesus who is giving me His love for each person I meet, even the strangers who come into my shop. I am not pious, I don't know how to pray very well, but I love Gospa so much, I speak to her about everything; and God, I love Him even more. My life breathes joy and love of God beyond words." (E, December 15, 1997).

A *preference*

Raphaëlle, a 7-year-old girl, prayed a novena to Mary for her first communion.

One morning her mother who was irritable from a night of insomnia, threatened her daughter who seemed about to misbehave:

— "Be careful or I'll deprive you of what you like the most."

— "You can't do that!" answered the child.

— "You'll go without ice cream!"

— "That's not what I love the most. It's God and you'll never be able to take Him away from me."

A *well-hidden fast*

Monique, who has discovered the messages of Medjugorje, decides to live the five points, but two of them worry her. She thus addresses Mary.

— "I promise to fast on Fridays. Please arrange for my son and my husband who are non-practising not to notice, because I am unable to face their comments."

The next Friday she sat at the table as usual, and ate two slices of bread. Nothing was said, either at dinner or supper. For more than two years, she fasted without anyone noticing. Later, when a criticism was finally made, Monique was strong enough to explain her fast. She has been able to continue with peace and joy.

"Decide to live what Mary is asking of you. Give her the part which your poverty prevents you from doing and you will always be a winner with Mary," concludes Sister Emmanuel (August 15, 1997).

Beyond snoring, grace

During his first night in Medjugorje, a pilgrim shared a room with an overweight man whose snoring was incredibly loud. The roommate tried all the old classics: whistling, making noise but nothing worked. The other chap just kept on snoring.

Frustrated and tired, he got up, left the house and went up to the Podbrdo hill. There, on the site of the first apparitions, he began to pray. For the first time in his life, prayers he had never said rose in his heart. He prayed for his fellowmen well into the night. He prayed for all the situations in which human beings found themselves at that time — young people in discos, on the street, those on drugs, people in hospitals, the dying, the desperate who were tempted by suicide, etc. He prayed with all his heart for his brothers.

He told Marija: "For the first time in my life, I gave a whole night of prayers to Jesus in circumstances where I would never have done so before."

God even uses snorers to get people to pray. (E, November 1, 1997).

Helpers helped

Some Italians came to Medjugorje; their car broke down and refused to start up for the return trip. They tried everywhere to find a mechanic. No one was able to repair their vehicle.

As a last resort, they came to see Marija, hoping she would know a good mechanic. No, she knew of none, but during the conversation she learned that one of the pilgrims had not been to confession in 36 years and had refused to go while on this pilgrimage. Marija took advantage of the mechanical delay and sent him to Father Arcadius. At the time she was recounting this, she did not know if he had left the confessional yet.

"God does marvelous things, even using frustrating delays," concluded Marija. Watch for them and see the graces hidden behind them (E, November 1, 1997).

5. RADIANCE

The theologian pilgrim

At the end of a letter, a theologian used some telegraphic words to recall his pilgrimage to Medjugorje (October 13, 1997):

— Confession, Way of the Cross, rosaries, conversation, prayer, silence during meals, meetings with Jelena and her father. (We lodged with Jelena).

On thursday, October 2nd, we happened to be at the blue Cross when Mirjana came with her husband and their eldest daughter for an apparition at 10:30 a.m. Upon leaving, she squeezed the arm of one of our friends from Le Havre and said to her: *"Deo gratias."* This was an unforgettable memory for our friend.

We were in awe of the Lord's work in the Cenacle Community (Sister Elvira's ex-drug-addicts).

The last day, under the tent, Father Slavko gave a teaching. I was filled with gratitude (E).

Our Lady of Medjugorje at the Congress in Washington

Mr. Tom Lantos, an influential Congressman in Washington DC, leader of the Human Rights Group, member of the *Commission for International Relations*, recognized the impact of the messages of peace of Medjugorje while listening to Sister Emmanuel in her weekly series on American television (1997). Although a Jew and not a Christian, he understood that Medjugorje was an important factor for peace in the world today. He asked Sister Emmanuel to come and speak in Washington on October 22, 1997, with this encouragement:

> *As we near the end of this millennium, we must gather a maximum amount of information on the means of living in peace and harmony. We will be happy to hear Sister Emmanuel speak to us of the fascinating and marvelous events of Medjugorje and the hopes for peace and reconciliation that they represent for the world.* (Dossier sent to us by Denis Nolan, organizer of this meeting, see chapter 5).

Congressman Lantos

Sister Emmanuel gave this information on the unfolding of the meeting:

Congressman Smith

— Our mission, *Message of Peace*, unfolded in the House of Congress in Washington DC on October 22, 1997. We were five members from the *Children of Medjugorje*, including Denis and Cathy Nolan, and the local representatives. Congressman Chris Smith, deeply involved with the protection of human life, welcomed us warmly. Thirty people came to hear the witnessing and messages of Medjugorje. The attendance was well representative of the local population: Christians,

Jews, Muslims, and some with no religion at all, but searching for true peace. Five or six members of Congress were mixed in with the other guests. The small group allowed for an intimate meeting. At the end of the presentation we had a good laugh, for all of our five watches started to ring at the same time — it was the moment of the apparition in Medjugorje! They were set to remind us every day of the event. One of the congressmen suggested that we pray. Those few minutes for God were undoubtedly the most important. I sincerely believe that Jesus and His Mother made an impression in that impressive *Capitol Building*. The elbow rubbing and the meal allowed for providential exchanges.

I will never be able to thank enough those who prayed and fasted for our intention. We saw new doors open up due to the graces of Medjugorje [...] We must continue to intervene for the American government, that it renew its motto: *In God we trust*. Medjugorje spreads love of life and respect for God's commandments. May the USA listen to the voice of Mary and stop all projects against life, for they only lead to a false peace (NM, December 1997, p. 7).

Pilgrimages

Fabienne Costermans, sister of Jacques, founder of *Nouvelles de Medjugorje*, relates how she left for Herzegovina without the least enthusiasm:

— To go to Medjugorje to fast and pray non-stop for a whole week is not a picnic! It will be difficult and trying.

Well, it was not at all!

The fasting required by the Queen of Peace in Medjugorje does not consist in "having one's stomach in one's heels," but to relearn to live in simplicity and to love the bread of the Eucharist more. And so it is a fast on bread and water (as much as we like) or with black tea, which helps to eliminate toxins. [I am less convinced of that notion, stimulants are contrary to the spirit of fasting.]

I felt joyful and I found true rest in God. When we give Him all our securities, he fills us beyond our expectations and at a place where we least expect it.

I spent the first two days sleeping. Then my body found its youthfulness again. I found myself running up and down hills with as much ease as that of a little goat. What is the strongest is what happens in one's heart.

How is it possible that, within such a short time, so many souls are coverted, reaffirmed, comforted! Only God can accomplish such wonders and marvels. Let us first seek the Kingdom of God and all the rest will be given to us in abundance! (NM December 1997, p. 8).

Chapter 7

MESSAGES

The parish of Medjugorje does not take into consideration the messages of the 25th of each month. We mention the others so that nothing of the story is lost. We reproduce the monthly messages without repeating each time the stereotypical formula: *"Dear children, today...Thank you for responding to my call."*

1997

January 25th, to Marija: *I invite you to reflect about your future. You are creating a new world without God, only with your own strength and that is why you are unsatisfied and without joy in the heart. This time is my time and that is why, little children, I invite you again to pray. When you find unity with God, you will feel hunger for the word of God and your heart, little children, will overflow with joy. You will witness God's love wherever you are. I bless you and I repeat to you that I am with you to help you.*

February 25th: *Today I invite you in a special way to open yourselves to God the Creator and to become active. I invite you, little children, to see at this time who needs your spiritual or material help. By your example, little children, you will be the extended hands of God, which humanity is seeking. Only in this way will you* *understand, that you are called to witness and to become joyful carriers of God's word and of His love.*

March 25th: *Today, in a special way, I invite you to take the cross in the hands and to meditate on the wounds of Jesus. Ask of Jesus to heal your wounds, which you, dear children, during your life sustained because of your sins or the sins of your parents. Only in this way, dear children, you will understand that the world is in need of healing of faith in God the Creator. By Jesus' passion and death on the cross, you will understand that only through prayer you, too, can become true apostles of faith; when, in simplicity and prayer, you live faith which is a gift.*

April 25th: *Today I call you to have your life be connected with God the Creator, because only in this way will your life have meaning and you will comprehend that God is love. God sends me to you out of love, that I may help you to comprehend that without Him there is no future or joy and, above all, there is no eternal salvation. Little children, I call you to leave sin and to accept prayer at all times, that you may in prayer come to know the meaning of your life. God gives Himself to him who seeks Him.*

May 25th: *Today I invite you to glorify God and for the Name of God to be holy in your hearts and in your life. Little children, when you are in the holiness of God, He is with you and gives you peace and joy which come from God only through prayer. That is why, little children, renew prayer in your families and your heart will glorify the holy Name of God and heaven will reign in your heart. I am close to you and I intercede for you before God.*

June 25th: *Today I am with you in a special way and I bring you my motherly blessing of peace. I pray for you and I intercede for you before God, so that you may comprehend that each of you is a carrier of peace. You cannot have peace if your heart is not at peace with God. That is why, little children, pray, pray, pray, because prayer is the* foundation of your peace. Open your heart and give time to God so that He will be your friend. When true friendship with God is realized, no storm can destroy it.

July 25th: *Today I invite you to respond to my call to prayer. I desire, dear children, that during this time you find a corner for personal prayer. I desire to lead you towards prayer with the heart. Only in this way will you comprehend that your life is empty without prayer. You will discover the meaning of your life when you discover God in prayer. That is why, little children, open the door of your heart and you will comprehend that prayer is joy without which you cannot live.*

August 25th: *God gives me this time as a gift to you, so that I may instruct and lead you on the path of salvation. Dear children, now you do not comprehend this grace, but soon a time will come when you will lament for these messages. That is why, little children, live all of the words which I have given you through this time of grace and renew prayer, until prayer becomes a joy for you. Especially, I call all those who have consecrated themselves to my Immaculate Heart to become an example to others. I call all priests and religious brothers and sisters to pray the rosary and to teach others to pray. The rosary, little children, is especially dear to me. Through the rosary open your heart to me and I am able to help you.*

September 25th: *Today I call you to comprehend that without love you cannot comprehend that God needs to be in the first place in your life. That is why, little children, I call you all to love, not with a human but with God's love. In this way, your life will be more beautiful and without an interest. You will comprehend that God gives Himself to you in the simplest way out of love. Little children, so that you may comprehend my words which I give you out of love, pray, pray, pray and you will be able to accept others with love and to forgive all who have done evil to you. Respond with prayer; prayer is a fruit of love towards God the Creator.*

October 25th: *Also today I am with you and I call all of you to renew yourselves by living my messages. Little children, may prayer be life for you and may you be an example to others. Little children, I desire for you to become carriers of peace and of God's joy to today's world without peace. That is why, little children, pray, pray, pray! I am with you and I bless you with my motherly peace.*

November 25th: *Today I invite you to comprehend your Christian vocation. Little children, I led and am leading you through this time of grace, that you may become conscious of your Christian vocation. Holy martyrs died witnessing: I am a Christian and love God over everything. Little children, today also I invite you to rejoice and be joyful Christians, responsible and conscious that God called you in a special way to be joyfully extended hands toward those who do not believe, and that through the example of your life, they may receive faith and love for God. Therefore, pray, pray, pray that your heart may open and be sensitive for the Word of God.*

December 25th: *Also today I rejoice with you and I call you to the good. I desire that each of you reflect and carry peace in your heart and say: I want to put God in the first place in my life. In this way, little children, each of you will become holy. Little children, tell everyone, I want the good for you and he will respond with the good and, little children, good will come to dwell in the heart of each man. Little children, tonight I bring to you the good of my Son who gave His life to save you. That is why, little children, rejoice and extend your hands to Jesus who is only good.*

1998

January 25th: *Today again I call all of you to prayer. Only with prayer, dear children, will your heart change, become better, and be more sensitive to the Word of God. Little children, do not permit Satan to pull you apart and* *to do with you what he wants. I call you to be responsible and determined and to consecrate each day to God in prayer. May Holy Mass, little children, not be a habit for you, but life. By living Holy Mass each day, you will feel the need for holiness and you will grow in holiness. I am close to you and intercede before God for each of you, so that He may give you strength to change your heart.*

February 25th: *Also today I am with you and I, again, call all of you to come closer to me through your prayers. In a special way, I call you to renunciation in this time of grace. Little children, meditate on and live, through your little sacrifices, the passion and death of Jesus for each of you. Only if you come closer to Jesus will you comprehend the immeasurable love He has for each of you. Through prayer and your renunciation you will become more open to the gift of faith and love towards the Church and the people who are around you. I love you and bless you.*

March 25th: *Also today I call you to fasting and renunciation. Little children, renounce that which hinders you from being closer to Jesus. In a special way I call you: Pray, because only through prayer will you be able to overcome your will and discover the will of God even in the smallest things. By your daily life, little children, you will become an example and witness that you live for Jesus or against Him and His will. Little children, I desire that you become apostles of love. By loving, little children, it will be recognized that you are mine.*

April 25th: *Today I call you, through prayer, to open yourselves to God as a flower opens itself to the rays of the morning sun. Little children, do not be afraid. I am with you and I intercede before God for each of you so that your heart receives the gift of conversion. Only in this way, little children, will you comprehend the importance of grace in these times and God will become nearer to you.*

May 25th: *Today I call you, through prayer and sacrifice, to prepare yourselves for the coming of the Holy Spirit. Little children, this is a time of grace and so, again, I call you to decide for God the Creator. Allow Him to transform and change you. May your heart be prepared to listen to, and live, everything which the Holy Spirit has in His plan for each of you. Little children, allow the Holy Spirit to lead you on the way of truth and salvation towards eternal life.*

June 25th: *Today I desire to thank you for living my messages. I bless you all with my motherly blessing and I bring you all before my Son Jesus.*

July 25th: *Today, little children, I invite you, through prayer, to be with Jesus, so that through a personal experience of prayer you may be able to discover the beauty of God's creatures. You cannot speak or witness about prayer, if you do not pray. That is why, little children, in the silence of the heart, remain with Jesus, so that He may change and transform you with His love. This, little children, is a time of grace for you. Make good use of it for your personal conversion, because when you have God, you have everything.*

August 25th: *Today I invite you to come still closer to me through prayer. Little children, I am your mother, I love you and I desire that each of you be saved and thus be with me in Heaven. That is why, little children, pray, pray, pray until your life becomes prayer.*

September 25th: *Today, I call you to become my witnesses by living the faith of your fathers. Little children, you seek signs and messages and do not see that, with every morning sunrise, God calls you to convert and to return to the way of truth and salvation. You speak much, little children, but you work little on your conversion. That is why, convert and start to live my messages, not with your words but with your life. In this way, little children, you will have the strength to decide for the true conversion of the heart.*

October 25th: *Today I call you to come closer to my Immaculate Heart. I call you to renew in your families the fervor of the first days when I called you to fasting, prayer and conversion. Little children, you accepted my messages with open hearts, although you did not know what prayer was. Today, I call you to open yourselves completely to me so that I may transform you and lead you to the heart of my son Jesus, so that He can fill you with His love. Only in this way, little children, will you find true peace - the peace that only God gives you.*

November 25th: *Today I call you to prepare yourselves for the coming of Jesus. In a special way, prepare your hearts. May holy Confession be the first act of conversion for you and then, dear children, decide for holiness. May your conversion and decision for holiness begin today and not tomorrow. Little children, I call you all to the way of salvation and I desire to show you the way to Heaven. That is why, little children, be mine and decide with me for holiness. Little children, accept prayer with seriousness and pray, pray, pray.*

December 25th: *In this Christmas joy I desire to bless you with my blessing. In a special way, little children, I give you the blessing of little Jesus. May He fill you with His peace. Today, little children, you do not have peace and yet you yearn for it. That is why, with my Son Jesus, on this day I call you to pray, pray, pray, because without prayer you do not have joy or peace or a future. Yearn for peace and seek it, for God is true peace.*

1999

January 25th: *I again invite you to prayer. You have no excuse to work more because nature still lies in deep sleep. Open yourselves in prayer. Renew prayer in your families. Put Holy Scripture in a visible place in your families, read it, reflect on it and learn how God loves His people. His love shows itself also in present times because He sends me to call you upon the path of salvation.*

February 25th: *Also today I am with you in a special way contemplating and living the passion of Jesus in my heart. Little children, open your hearts and give me everything that is in them: joys, sorrows and each, even the smallest, pain, that I may offer them to Jesus; so that with His immeasurable love, He may burn and transform your sorrows into the joy of His resurrection. That is why, I now call you in a special way, little children, for your hearts to open to prayer, so that through prayer you may become friends of Jesus.*

March 25th: *I call you to prayer with the heart. In a special way, little children, I call you to pray for conversion of sinners, for those who pierce my heart and the heart of my Son Jesus with the sword of hatred and daily blasphemies. Let us pray, little children, for all those who do not desire to come to know the love of God, even though they are in the Church. Let us pray that they convert, so that the Church may resurrect in love. Only with love and prayer, little children, can you live this time which is given to you for conversion. Place God in the first place, then the risen Jesus will become your friend.*

April 25th: *Also today, I call you to prayer. Little children, be joyful carriers of peace and love in this peaceless world. By fasting and prayer, witness that you are mine and that you live my messages. Pray and seek! I am praying and interceding for you before God that you convert; that your life and behavior always be Christian.*

— Chapter 8 —
CONCLUSION

In conclusion, I dedicate this book and what it recounts as a thanksgiving to Our Lady for so much good fruit. These fruits are the conversions and healings, for which Christians give thanks. There are more abundant confessions than any other place in the world: daily, persevering, and at what cost for the confessors who assume this huge task in spite of so many contradictions.

Thanksgiving

The *Queen of Peace committee* gives thanks, for during the war, the bombs which destroyed so much elsewhere spared this fragile village and prized target. One bomb exploded outside the village, killing only a cow and a chicken. On the contrary, Citluk, its neighbor, was severely hit. We must give thanks especially for the private humanitarian aid, unequalled in generosity, and unassuming in character, often taken from door to door, and ecumenical, including to Muslims. Some volunteer rescuers gave their lives in the effort.

This supposedly pietistic movement developed humanitarian and social dimensions which we dealt with in chapter 5, and which continue to this day, at a time when Bosnia is left to its own sad destiny.

Where else have we seen such complete development of all human and Christian values, and this straightforward opening up to our youth, so neglected, so abandoned and who undertake this uncomfortable journey to fast and to pray (see above chapter 5).

The converts and apostolic leaders are amazed that this fruitful zeal is so opposed and pushed into the background, while so many cultural activities, sometimes against the faith, are encouraged as if spiritual discernment had been forgotten.

In spite of this restrictive situation, as men of God and fathers to their flock, many bishops have discovered in their own dioceses the flow of graces emanating from this remote center, with faith, charity and human and Christian commitment. Will they intervene in order to put an end to this quarantine?

Unless the grain dies

Our Lady's dominion has been severely tried by the Marxist State. Even in the Church at times, the grace of God and holiness do not prevent unjust persecutions or the exclusion of founders and troublesome mystics (Padre Pio, etc.). This has caused one of my friends from Marseilles to say that there are three types of saints. (I have removed the first two epithets of his colourful comment): persecuting saints, persecuted saints and happy saints of whom he is one. How can we not categorize as persecutors those Franciscans who wrongly installed microphones in Padre Pio's confessional? How about those in Medjugorje who have maintained the peace, the pastoral care and the primacy of spiritual matters amid so much repression and opposition, and who have been subjected to retaliation after retaliation?

First came the communist persecution and the imprisonment of Father Jozo Zovko and of many parishioners, not to mention the condemnation with fines and prohibition from staying in Medjugorje for the author of this book.

Then came the opposition from those with ecclesiastic authority who never ceased obstructing the pastoral response to the immense responsibility of caring for souls. Happily, the spokesman for Rome recently proclaimed that priests accompanying private pilgrimages were desirable for spiritual guidance, the administration of sacraments, and confessions. This contradicts the negative propaganda of apparently quasi-official declarations (chapter 3, p. 33).

In 1985, during one of the moments of crises, the parish as a whole presented its case to the Holy See. The dignified and detailed letter, signed by all the representatives, was sent to seven major Roman offices. (DN 6, p. 33). To this date, they have yet to receive a single reply. Why are some groups ignored by the Church?

Two Franciscan priests were slapped with multiple measures which were subsequently declared null, and illegal, by the supreme Tribunal of the Church after eight years. During that time justice had been irregularly held up, as we saw on p. 84 and DN 13, p. 47-50.

Confronted with this plethora of hardships and opposition from the communist government as well as from high authorities within the Church, I foresaw in 1984 a gloomy future, at least from a human perspective. These situations usually provoke common revolt or annihilation, exaltation or divergence, clarification or depression. Thus ended a great many fervent charismatic movements, from Montanism (2nd to 4th centuries) to small medieval groups, not to mention the crisis of the Great Reformation (R. Laurentin, *L'Esprit Saint*, volume 12, p. 201-288).

To date, grace has always proven to be the strongest in Medjugorje. The Franciscan parish has persevered peacefully in its impossible spiritual task, adding to the daily service of its own parishioners the responsibility for the international pilgrimages, the dimension of which are parallel to those of Fatima. All this is done without official status, without help from the Church, and without suitable quarters or the authorization to build new ones. Father Orec, who undertook the task under pressing conditions, was quickly transferred and stripped of any canonical commission in the diocese of Mostar.

The parish has never fallen into the trap of retaliating against the provocations, including one handed to it by a homily of Bishop Zanic against the apparitions. It occurred under the guise of a confirmation ceremony in Medjugorje. He sought to provoke the hot-headed Croats so that they might be accused of a scandalous revolt against the Bishop. This tactic might have succeeded elsewhere, but the parishioners of Medjugorje, taught by Our Lady, knew how to listen without protest. They heroically overcame the interior shock, out of respect for the apostolic authority. This brought the Bishop to another conclusion that supported his thesis: "See," he said to the Franciscans, "they don't believe anymore." (DN 7, p. 72-75; cf 9, 147).

Outside of Medjugorje, others did not possess the same heroism. The caring for souls, the assistance to those excluded from the urgent request for the sacraments, moved some priests to disobey the Bishop and take their ministry to the striking parishioners.

Disobedience is always an error, but why provoke unnecessary and foreseeable rebellion, foment their decay and prolong sanctions which push fervent priests out of the Church. It is as if someone wanted to prove that Franciscans, though exemplary in Medjugorje, are not true men of God, but serious delinquents. It is not good that the law should increasingly lead to disorder and sin — we should go beyond that and live by the law of love, according to St. Paul.

— "You are degrading your episcopal office," wrote the future Cardinal Urs von Balthasar to Bishop Zanic.

Urs von Balthasar

That was too severe, for Bishop Zanic was a dignified bishop. But those in authority must not give the appearance of denying fundamental truths which are the basis of faith itself, according to the Second Vatican Council:

> God is love,
>
> the Church is communion,
>
> authority is collegiality,
>
> her function is to preside in charity,
>
> to animate the love, and the life which is the essence of the Church.

Medjugorje can give thanks to Our Lady for obtaining a profusion of marvellous wonders while at the same time dodging the worst that I could humanly foresee at the time of Bishop Zanic's negative judgement. I related at the time how I would obey for good order without denying anything that I had written objectively, for it seemed improbable and contrary to usual practice that Cardinal Ratzinger would reject the negative judgement firmly proposed by the local bishop (DN 5, 53-56; 7, 10-16). Monsignor Zanic, man of worth, but hot-blooded and impulsive, had proceeded too quickly. The method of the successor he designated to replace him is to act calmly on all fronts: Roman, legal, and moderate, emanating from the Holy See itself. The negative judgement will fall like a ripe fruit.

The movement of prayer and action, profound and liturgical, traditional and generous (which opponents characterized as superficial, illuminist, even superstitious), is an austere movement.

The prayers of the pilgrims crammed standing up inside a church which is too small, where we pray and preach in a language they do not understand, should create a void which unfortunately is evident in regular, comfortable churches... However, in Medjugorje, prayer and meditation is prolonged long after the lengthy services. This also thwarts all anticipated results and prognostications. I have less stamina and energy than that mass of tireless pilgrims.

Is it then fitting that the misinformation end up by quarantining Medjugorje more and more, discredited by systematic private and sometimes official actions (chapters 3-4)?

Will the Pope who is privately favorable, put into place a peace and reconciliation process for the service of spiritual affairs, and to do this in spite of those who harden the conflict to finally bring about the elimination of the Franciscans from that province where the flourishing novitiate was dissolved?

We must give thanks to Our Lady, because to date everything has worked together to the benefit of the sanctuary, even the errors, exterior and interior: the spittle of slander belongs on the surface, producing patience and heroic perseverance.

The trial is not over. It has never been so severe.

Will Our Lady triumph in Medjugorje? We must hope so. But her ardent prayer did not save Her Son from death. It served only to prepare His Resurrection and what followed.

Prayer is the only way out (in full respect of authority). Pilgrims pray with fervor for the solution. That is how to overcome temptations, which provoke so many anomalies. Pilgrims hope for a better fate than Christ's before human authorities, or that of Joan of Arc before Bishop Cauchon and his tribunal, which was scrupulously constituted according to all the standards of the law.

Any war between the canonical and the spiritual should never arise in the Church. Following the norms, so clear in the Gospel, any conflict or difference must be resolved in peace, through love, as we saw in the quarrel of the early community over the Greek widows (Acts 6), or with the first east-west quarrel at the time of St. Irenee. Evil will prevail when the two factors are split apart. They exasperate each other in a fratricidal war, when the law which is normally right, transforms itself into a war machine to combat the works of God, be it ever so fruitful.

The Bishop of Mostar has asked me to be silent concerning Medjugorje. He did not give me an order, knowing full well as a canonist, that he did not have the power to do so. I am grateful to him for this lawfulness.

This request seemed to be providential at a time when the works of truth sink deeper into conflict, and removes from me any possibility of being understood. Those in authority show themselves to be more and more clearly opposed to Medjugorje. I will go no further into that degrading conflict, where I would risk degrading myself, my objective point of view bringing criticism to those people I still respect and value. I feel sorry for those who are called by their vocation to be involved with this willfully corrupt situation in which I tried to help. It has also become impossible for me to be of assistance now that my adversaries have sullied my reputation, which had been well established.

According to law, the bishop contests the presence of many communities, and does not grant any canonical mission to the young Franciscans formed in the novitiate in Humac which has been shut down. The way out of such a conflict would be with an "I accuse", which would be so easy to do. It would target the entire conscientious bureaucratic system, where slander, not formation, is cultivated, division rather than peace, the negative rather than the fruit, where those responsible hide within the knots of a complex power system. That system has been promoting inextricable divisions and darkness in this diocese for half a century. It supports those who solidify combative authoritarianism and hardens those who dare follow an objective discernment as I tried to do, or separate themselves from the Church or even revolt against it, as often happens, giving their authorized adversaries victory over them.

All of this multiplies conscientious objectors. This is unhealthy, as it stifles the movement of grace and the response to the appeal to souls from which well-founded motives for conversion are stripped (DN 4, p. 27-33). That is how Bishop Cauchon prepared a perfect canonical scheme against Joan of Arc and was then able to wash his hands of it. His tribunal was rigorously legal, and it was the secular arm which burned Joan of Arc at the stake. The only thing left to do was to give thanks for this solution, which eliminated the body by fire.

The most ambiguous part of this drama is that we are not exactly certain where responsible decisions are taken for each case. The bishop makes few decisions. The Franciscans make many more, but in many cases, they are invited by a superior authority to make these decisions in their own name like the old system which used to work and which Vatican II has greatly reformed. Today, the authorities of the Church ask to be forgiven for errors of the distant past. What is more important is not to repeat those same errors.

Bishop Peric greeted me courteously and amiably. For that I am grateful. I had hoped that my free and respectful acceptance of his request for my silence would contribute to peace, and this, together with my request for him to take into consideration the spiritual fruit, and to place his pastoral office at the service of this fruit. The first fax I received, on the following day, was a disappointment. I had asked for a private meeting in order to better understand and serve the bishop who is Jesus' authority in the Church. That visit, where I had little opportunity to do anything but to listen, and make a maximum effort to approach the Bishop's point of view, was concluded with a public communiqué against me, riddled with personal observations and epithets, distorting and caricaturing my comments. It was made much easier for him because I had not sought to defend myself during this visit, but rather sought understanding and unity, mixed with discreet petitions.

Another fax received the same day alerted me squarely and more acutely that this visit was the prelude to a much harder fight against me personally. By showing signs of weakness, I left myself in for the kill. By seeking peace, I fell into a trap.

I was tempted not to confirm my resolution to stop my annual series of information books. I do persist in my decision for the sake of peace, hoping that my demobilization will not be another factor in the hardening of the resolve against me, and especially against the grace which has continued to flow in Medjugorje for the last 17 years.

TESTAMENT

This being my time of testament, I present here not my last will, for I have no other will but God's and the Church's. This will is not always easy to clarify, but much hope is placed on the Lord.

Pilgrims, continue to pray in this oasis of grace, which is open to private pilgrimages as Rome has confirmed. Persevere with full respect for the authorities, beginning with the local bishop, as you have done thus far, so that God may bless him and guide his actions as successor of the apostles.

Be humble, obedient and persevering, even under aggression, opposition or provocation that can erode your communion in the Church.

You, who have in your hand the Authority of the Lord, keep as your priority the promotion of faith and love, to serve the Lord and Our Lady as you love them. Do not abandon yourselves to power that corrupts, but to the evangelistic authority which presides with charity. May it overcome passions, and inspire administrative solutions that are constructive and fruitful.

Do not close your eyes to the flow of grace, which is without equal in the Church today, at least as pertains to the conversions, and the confessions, and the healings for which many give thanks to God.

"Do not stifle the Holy Spirit," as Paul exhorts us (1 Thess. 5, 19). Do not foster but extinguish everything that incites conflicts and sins. Make yourself loved by a renewed understanding of spiritual matters, and of sincere souls.

You who tolerate and support so many institutions where prayer is disappearing, where faith and sometimes morals are disintegrating, where vocations are few or are lost, do not fight against this unequalled source of conversions and vocations.

You who, according to the doctrines of the Church and of the Bible, are respectful of life in all its forms, and discourage abortions, do not perpetrate abortion of this great grace.

See the disarray of so many converts of Medjugorje who do not understand why we quarrel, and question what has been for them an oasis of light and a rebirth in Christ Jesus. Do not scandalize these little ones, for your mission is to make peace and not to crush your adversaries.

Put forth, as I have been suggesting for so many years, a true peace process. Renew the dialogue, as most developed secular nations do today. They push dialogue endlessly in order to resolve violent and inextricable conflicts. Be inspired by the Gospel.

Entrust this dialogue to Spirit-filled people and not to hardened canonists or the elite.

Do not multiply negative actions, which create irregularities, as though to finally allow a generalized repression and a death warrant for Our Lady of Medjugorje.

Patiently remedy what is less good by supporting what is good, rather than neutralizing it. Prepare for the future.

If possible, send mediators who are primarily spiritual men of peace, capable of finding the solutions sought in vain for the last half-century.

Allow the Franciscans to build a church in proportion to the size of the crowds; help them to better distribute their energies between the pilgrims and the parish, which overwork causes them to neglect, except for the short winter months (January and February).

Do not discredit the healings that doctor Korljan has recognized in accordance with his official mission. As well, do not upset the visionaries' equilibrium.

Do not dissuade the pilgrimages which have borne so many conversions and spiritual discoveries for the service of the Church. Do not uproot this garden of graces which has played such a providential role in the present conflict in the Church and against the invasion of sects.

Do not perpetuate the obstinacy of the scribes and Pharisees about which the Gospel of the man born blind gives such a clear lesson.

Promote peace and not war. Do not prevent priests from discerning grace and serving it, where they perceive it objectively along with hundreds of Catholic bishops.

Foster reconciliation.

Learn how to find new avenues of understanding and edification which will lead you to be loved by those whom you love, rising above conflicts and trials which they have difficulty in comprehending.

This is important at a time when too many people who still love Christ do not know how to love the Church which shows them the grim face of a mother who is unheeding, scolding and punitive. Help the Church to be loved, and be loved yourselves by those who will love you with all the more joy and fruit when you show them the face of Christ.

Chapter 9

APPENDICES

MONSIGNOR PERIC'S POSITION

To all lords, all honor. Bishop Peric has published:

1. A book, *Prijestojle Mudrosti* (*The Seat of Wisdom*) Mostar 1995, pp. 266-286, with a conclusive chapter against Medjugorje. He concludes against but with a concern for moderation, which honors him.

2. His letter to *Famille Chrétienne* is more exhaustive. He encourages the struggle for the annihilation of Medjugorje's credit amongst the Christian elite, which honors this publication.

1. THE SEAT OF WISDOM

The phenomenon of Medjugorje and the Church's declarations

Since 1981 three ecclesiastic commissions have successively studied the phenomenon of Medjugorje, [...] sent out communiqués or explanations which the proponents or adversaries of the "supernatural apparitions" accept or reject.

Here are the most important developments. They are dated and signed by the competent authorities:

1. In mid-*August 1981*, a declaration from Pavao Zanic, Bishop of Mostar-Duvno, left the door open for a favorable interpretation, saying: "The most difficult question remains whether this is the subjective experience of children or something supernatural."

2. On *January 14, 1984*, Cardinal Franjo Kuharic, Archbishop of Zagreb, prohibited the visionaries from speaking in all the parishes of the diocese of Zagreb until an ecclesiastic judgement of the events was established.

3. On *March 24, 1984*, the first communiqué of the "enlarged" commission was made public. The commission asked the mass media to refrain from judging the events until the competent commission had passed judgement.

It also asked that the organization of pilgrimages not be authorized, or that the "visionaries" and the servants of the church in Medjugorje make no declaration on the supposed "apparitions." "The events of Medjugorje have created a considerable echo in our local Church and around the world. The local ordinary has deemed it necessary to enlarge the commission presently made up of four members. This way new members will be chosen from all the theology faculties of the Church of Croatia and Slovenia. They will include diverse theological disciplines and experts in medical sciences... *The commission does not approve the organization of pilgrimages to Medjugorje by Catholic priests or the laity, nor public presentations of the visionaries, before it has rendered a judgement on the authenticity of the apparitions.*"[1]

4. On *October 11, 1984*, the second communiqué indicated, amongst other things: "The commission has decided to extend the study of the children's experiences and the interpretation of these experiences by the pastors of

Medjugorje. It already notes certain difficulties of disciplinary and theological order in the messages of Medjugorje."[2]

5. On *October 12, 1984*, the *Episcopal Conference* asked that *official pilgrimages* be not organized in Medjugorje. "The bishops warn that, concerning the events of Medjugorje, it is necessary to await the judgement of the Church's competent authorities, which will be pronounced after a complete and pertinent examination of the events. Consequently, official pilgrimages to Medjugorje cannot be organized as if the Church had already pronounced a positive judgement on the events."[3]

6. On *October 30, 1984*, Bishop Zanic presented the position (non-official) of the diocesan chancellery in a 15-point statement, defining the negative factors and facts linked to the Medjugorje phenomenon. [4]

7. On *March 8, 1985*, the commission's third communiqué on the conclusions of the experts and the studies were made public. It said, notably: "The commission believes that the most difficult question arising from the events concerns the ecclesiastic disobedience of two ex-chaplains from Mostar who refused to be transferred, invoking the messages of Medjugorje."[5]

8. On *April 18, 1985*, the Episcopal Conference once again published an appeal to the faithful against official pilgrimages to Medjugorje: "The bishops are closely following the events of Medjugorje in Herzegovina. During their meeting, they reiterated their previous directives and decisions concerning these events."

9. On *May 23, 1985*, came the warning by the Congregation for the Doctrine of Faith — signed by the Congregation secretary, Monsignor Alberto Bovone — addressed to the *Italian Episcopal Conference*, not to organize pilgrimages to Medjugorje. Here is the complete text of that letter: [...]

"Your Excellency, from all sides we note and deplore — and in particular the competent Ordinary of Mostar

(Yugoslavia) — the vast propaganda around the facts linked to the supposed apparitions in Medjugorje. Pilgrimages and other initiatives have been launched, which can only contribute to the spreading of confusion among the faithful and to impede the delicate examination of the facts, which the commission is striving to conclude. In order to avoid the extension of this propaganda and the speculation it is provoking in Italy, this Presidency (of the Italian Episcopal Conference) deems to suggest to the Italian episcopate to discourage the public organization of pilgrimages to the alleged apparition center. The same is said for all other forms of publicity, especially in written form, which would be considered prejudicial to a serene examination of the facts by the special commission, which was canonically constituted for that purpose. I take this opportunity to express the assurance of my highest consideration..."[6]

10. On *May 31, 1985*, the fourth communiqué of the diocesan commission presented the subjects and the difficulties it had examined:

— Comparison of the concept of conversion according to the Gospels and according to the phenomenon of Medjugorje;

— Problem of discipline concerning the two ex-chaplains of Mostar who appealed to the messages of Medjugorje;

— Theological problems with certain messages of Medjugorje;

— Insufficient documentation on the presumed miraculous healings."

11. On *September 27, 1985*, the fifth communiqué from the same commission briefly explained what the members were doing.[7]

12. In *January, 1987*, acting on the suggestion from the Congregation for the Doctrine of Faith that a commission

of experts be created at the level of the *Episcopal Conference*, a joint communication from Cardinal Kuharic and Bishop Zanic was published:

While we await the results of the Commission's studies and the judgement of the Church, the pastors and the faithful must observe an attitude of prudence, which is critical in such situations. It is hence not permitted to organize pilgrimages or other outward expressions, motivated by the supernatural character which could be attributed to the events in Medjugorje.[7]

13. On *January 25, 1987*, during a Mass in the parish of Medjugorje, Bishop Zanic referred to the alleged apparitions. The following paragraph was printed in numerous newspapers around the world. "We are told that Our Lady started to appear on Podbrdo on the hill of Crnica. When the police prohibited anyone from gathering there, Our Lady descended into the houses, in the gardens, in the fields, in the vineyards and in the tobacco fields. She appeared in the church, on the altar, in the sacristy, in the choir loft, on the roof and on the steeple. Next She appeared in the street, on the road to Cerno, in cars, on buses, on a train, in different places in Mostar, in Sarajevo, in the convent in Zagreb, in Varazdin, in Switzerland, in Italy and once again in the presbytery, etc. This list does not contain half of the alleged appearance sites, and a serious person who venerates Our Lady must ask himself: 'Holy Mother of God, what have they done with you?'"[9]

14. In *1990* Bishop Zanic published his position on Medjugorje in a text summarizing 28 points which had profoundly dissuaded him from considering as authentic the supposed supernatural apparitions as well as what is scandalizing many of the faithful, pertaining to the events of Medjugorje.[10]

15. On *April 10, 1991*, came the *Yugoslav Episcopal Conference*'s declaration on the results of the Commission, in which there existed no valid reason

that could allow for the belief in the events of Medjugorje, be they apparitions or revelations. Here is the complete text:

"The members of the Yugoslav *Episcopal Conference*, gathered in ordinary session on April 9, 10, 11, in Zadar, have agreed upon the following:[11]

The Bishop presents at this point the Zadar declaration printed in chapter 3, p. 40-41.

Later, war broke out in Croatia and Bosnia-Herzegovina. The supporters of the Medjugorje phenomenon persist in declaring that Our Lady continues to 'appear.'

The diocesan chancellery has repeatedly warned that we cannot proclaim nor preach the supernaturality of the apparitions in our churches since it is not possible to prove that Our Lady does appear. Hence, official pilgrimages to Medjugorje are not allowed.[12]"

Position of the diocese of Mostar-Duvno

The Church still has not recognized the supernatural character of the "apparitions" in Medjugorje.

Bearing in mind the rules mentioned earlier, the members of the Commission were invested with the responsibility of examining the phenomenon. They took under consideration that it was impossible to prove the supernatural character of the "apparitions." Also bearing in mind what had been said and written in the past and more recently pertaining to the parish of Medjugorje and the events involving it, *we present a few fundamental positions which the diocesan chancellery rendered public by different means. It informed the Holy See of these positions and continues to maintain them to this day.*

1. *The Herzegovina and Medjugorje quarrel.* From the beginning of the alleged apparitions, the Bishop of

Mostar, Monsignor Pavao Zanic was entirely disposed to welcoming the news in the diocese of Mostar-Duvno, in the parish of Medjugorje, that the Blessed Virgin Mary was appearing. When the alleged visionaries through the supposed messages they were receiving from Our Lady began to take sides and make declarations against the Church in the Herzegovina conflict over its parishes, of the territorial jurisdiction, of the canonical powers, and to support the disobedience of certain Franciscan pastors, prudence recommended that a more reserved position be taken.[13]

The competent authorities of the Church, starting with the diocesan bishop and the investigations of his two inquiry commissions in 1982 and 1986, followed by the *Episcopal Conference* and its investigations of 1987 and 1990, agreed to judge negatively the supernatural origins of the apparitions in Medjugorje. They stated: "It is not possible to confirm the apparitions or revelations as being supernatural, by Our Lady or any other saint."

For this reason it is not permitted to pretend or profess the contrary in churches or ecclesiastic communities, that Our Lady has appeared or is still appearing in Medjugorje.[14]

2. *The fruit.*[15] In spite of the crowds which come to Medjugorje "for reasons inherent to their faith or for other reasons," be they priests, bishops, religious, curious or those seeking physical healings and spiritual conversions, in spite of dozens of books and brochures favorable to the alleged apparitions of Medjugorje, all written by scholars or authors of world-class reputation, in spite of hundreds of thousands of confessions and communions which the advocates of Medjugorje underline abundantly, the *Episcopal Conference*'s declaration clearly indicates: "It is not possible to ascertain that these are supernatural apparitions or revelations of Our Lady."

The fruit, so often mentioned, does not prove that they derive from "supernatural apparitions or revelations" of Our Lady. As they are authentically Christian, they can be interpreted as being a product of the normal work of divine grace, by faith in God, through Our Lady's intercession and by the sacraments of the Catholic Church. All this without mentioning the negative fruit!

3. *The messages.*[16] The messages of Medjugorje on prayer, fasting, faith, conversion and peace, repeated daily as something new but in reality always the same, as if Our Lady was transmitting them to the "visionaries," are always present in Holy Scripture and the Magisterium of the Catholic Church. Whosoever wants to obey and live in conformity with the Ten Commandments of God and the teachings of the Church, can pray, fast, believe, convert and work for peace around the world. This duty of Christians cannot be diminished, added to, nor reinforced by a confirmed apparition, much less by the thousands of non-confirmed apparitions of Medjugorje.

4. *Contradictions.*[17] Among the assertions of the alleged visionaries of Medjugorje, published over the last 14 years, there exist such contradictions, falsehoods and other trivialities which could not be attributed to Our Heavenly Mother, *Sedes Sapientiae*, Seat of Wisdom, since they do not present a minimum of credibility. Confronted by these assertions and these events with which they are linked, it is impossible to ascertain that these are supernatural apparitions and revelations of Our Lady or any other saint. The "great sign" or "ten secrets" which Our Lady presumably related to the children, reminds us of the alarmist tactics which characterized some non-Catholic communities and are not the solid teachings of the Catholic Church.

5. *Normal persons.*[18] Of the six children at the beginning of Medjugorje who affirmed that Our Lady was

"appearing" to them, one has entered the seminary, another in a sort of mixed religious community. With time, both left their respective community. Five are now married, including the two mentioned above. These faithful, even after thousands of alleged apparitions, remain so normal in their conduct, that only their words attest to their "meetings" with Our Lady. They remain "normal" as are all other "normal" faithful who have never "seen" Our Lady and who nevertheless continue to believe in her and piously invoke her intercession.

Our holy faith, which rests on the Word of God and not on the vision of celestial apparitions, is an *"obsequium rationabile"* (Rom 12, 1), a reasonable homage, which contradicts the insistent propaganda of daily or very frequent apparitions. The conduct of some contradicts the beatitude which Jesus told an incredulous Thomas: "Blessed are they who have not seen and yet believe" (Jn 20, 29).

6. *Charitable activities.*[19] In spite of all the charitable and humanitarian aid, which came in during the terrible war which devastated my country, there is no reason to profess that the apparitions or revelations are supernatural, neither that of the "Queen of Peace" or any other person.

7. *Destroyed churches and intact churches.*[20] Neither can it be considered as proof of supernatural origin, the fact that the church of St. James of Medjugorje was not hit by projectiles during the war while two churches in Mostar and many others in Herzegovina, Bosnia and Croatia were destroyed.

8. *The unceasing "apparition" process.*[21] Those who proclaim that the "Queen of Peace" has been appearing daily for 14 years in Medjugorje (although it was said in 1981 that the apparitions would cease in three days' time), and do not know how to stop the apparition process without restraining the pilgrims, who are attracted by some alleged apparitions or for other

motives, render no service to Our Lady's honor and truth. They also render no service to the spiritual Mother of all Catholics who place their faith on God and their devotion to Mary not on childish stories or imaginings, but on the authentic Revelation of God, and on its authentic interpretation guaranteed by the Holy Spirit and received through the living Magisterium of the Church.

9. *Tourism.*[22] By stating that it is truly impossible to prove or affirm that the Blessed Virgin Mary has ever appeared to anyone in Medjugorje, we do not wish to discourage the efforts of the Republic, or of the media, to attract more tourists to our country. However, let those necessary and fruitful tourist objectives rest on our praiseworthy Christian traditions, and on the martyrs for the faith yesterday and today, along with the beauty and the attraction with which the Almighty has blessed our country. May those objectives not rest upon "apparitions," "revelations," and "messages" without consistency nor basis.

The Croatian civil authorities and the mass media will have to clearly establish a distinction between those facts, and bear in mind the official position of the Church if they wish to respect the principal of non-intervention in matters concerning the Church, and prove objectivity.

10. *Neither cult nor pilgrimage.* Neither the diocesan bishop as head of the Mostar-Duvno diocese, nor any other competent authority has ever officially declared the parish church of St. James of Medjugorje as a "Marian Sanctuary."[23] No "cult" of the Virgin Mary based on alleged apparitions was ever proclaimed.

Due to overlapping, the local Ordinary has on many occasions prohibited anyone from preaching in the churches on the supernatural origin of the alleged apparitions or revelations, and from organizing *official* pilgrimages, be they in the name of the parish, the diocese or the Church.

These warnings and other similar ones were formulated by the *Episcopal Conference of Yugoslavia* and by the Holy See. Whoever disregards these directives directly opposes the official declarations of the Church, which after 14 years of alleged apparitions and intensive propaganda, still remain valid for Catholics.

Conclusion [24]

A wholesome devotion to the Mother of God, in accordance with the teachings of the Church, notably in the papal exhortation of 1974 *"Marialis cultus"*, must be nourished and encouraged at the level of each person, each family, each parish, each diocese of the Catholic Church.

Mostar, May, 1995

Monsignor Ratko Peric
Bishop of Mostar

MONSIGNOR PERIC'S LETTER TO "FAMILLE CHRETIENNE"

This letter was published in volume 1 of *Edifa*, p. 92

Mostar, October 2, 1997

I am replying to your letter, dated 29/9/1997, received by fax at the Nunciature of Sarajevo.

Concerning the position of this diocese[25] with regards to the alleged apparitions or revelations in Medjugorje, especially the formula *"non constat de supernaturalitate"* or "notice of non-supernaturality," here is what I can declare:

1. The second diocesan commission which worked from 1984 to 1986, voted explicitly on May 2, 1986, in a crushing majority,[26] the *"non constat de supernaturalitate"* (11 negative votes, 2 positive and 1 "in nucleo", 1 abstention).

2. The *Episcopal Conference* in 1991 stated:

"On the basis of the investigations established to date, we cannot ascertain that the apparitions or revelations are supernatural."

3. The Congregation for the Doctrine of Faith, citing the complete declarations of the bishops of former Yugoslavia in two identical letters sent to two French prelates, Monsignor Daloz, Archbishop of Besançon (July 4, 1995) and Monsignor Tardivet, Bishop of Langres (March 23, 1996), states: "From all that has been said, it is evident that the pilgrimages to Medjugorje, understood as a site of true Marian apparitions, must not be organized from a parochial or diocesan level. They would be in contradiction with what has been affirmed by the bishops of the former Yugoslavia in their declaration".[27]

4. On the basis of the serious study of this case by thirty odd researchers (up to three commissions), of my 5 years of Episcopal experience in the diocese, of the *scandalous disobedience* which surrounds the phenomenon, of the *lies* that are placed in "Our Lady's" mouth, of the unusual *repetition* of the messages over sixteen years, of the manner in which the "spiritual directors" of the alleged "visionaries" take them around the world to stir up propaganda, of the principle of having "Our Lady" appearing at the *fiat* (let it be done) of the "visionaries,"[28]

My conviction and my position are not only *non constat de supernaturalitate*, but *Constat de nonsupernaturalitate* of the apparitions or revelations of Medjugorje.[29]

5. Nevertheless, I am open to any study that the Holy See, as Highest Authority in the Catholic Church, would choose to undertake to render a supreme and definitive judgement on this case[30] and all of this as soon as possible for the well being of souls, for the honor of the Church and that of Our Lady.

Monsignor Ratko Peric
Bishop of Mostar

INTERVIEW OF JELENA VASILJ BY ALBERTO BONIFACIO JANUARY 2, 1998

Jelena, a second generation visionary who does not have apparitions in the regular sense, that is exterior, objective, but sees and hears Gospa in her heart, spoke with Alberto Bonifacio who was questioning her on her experiences. Following a summary of the phenomenon, she answered his more specific questions in Italian.

Jelena Vasilj

I'll endeavor to tell you of my experience, although I've often repeated it. Afterwards, I'll answer your more specific questions.

My experience is not the same as that of the other visionaries. I have not had apparitions like theirs [...] but I can speak of a certain kind of vision. It is a rather unique grace, that of a particular presence of Mary through prayer. The Lord is always present in our prayer, but it seems that sometimes He decides to reveal Himself and to be felt more alive, as if a veil fell. The Lord then allows a small ray of light to reach us in prayer. Such is our experience: it is to feel Mary's presence quite strongly. It is an experience of the heart [...] not only an idea, a thought which enters, but the presence of a true Person. In order to truly meet another person, the Catechism of the Catholic Church teaches us, our heart must be open [...] Otherwise, prayer remains superficial. That is how it is with God in the true experience of prayer. The heart is truly implicated (coinvolto). That is why we speak of inner locution of the heart.

The experience began about 18 months after the beginning of the apparitions (hence end of 1982) with the experience of an angel, then Our Lady.

I consider the presence of the angel as a preparation for what was to follow because the first words of the angel were very significant for me. The first thing he asked me was to go to confession, followed by purity of heart that I might see him. I believe that the first step in a serious Christian life is forgiveness. Then Gospa teaches us to pray in this manner: we place ourselves in the presence of God; we beg His forgiveness and His mercy. It is the first step in our conversion. Two weeks later, I felt Our Lady's presence and sometimes Jesus'. Another girl from the group (prayer group) achieved this prayer and experience in March.

In the beginning, she felt Mary's presence but then in October of the same year, she began to receive messages. I believe it was more or less our role to receive those messages, those illuminations, those inspirations through prayer, and to communicate them especially to our prayer group, which Gospa asked us to organize here in the parish. We were about sixty young people and we tried as a group to deepen and live Our Lady's messages to the visionaries. The content of the messages we received in the group is not much different from those received by the others. It is mostly a way of prayer. Gospa always places prayer first because our Christian life takes its energy in that meeting with God. If there is no meeting with God, it is very difficult to speak of a spiritual life because it is not our work. [...] Very quickly in our Christian life we come to realize that we cannot do very much by ourselves and that it is grace that truly guides us.

That is why Gospa leads us to prayer: that prayer might become a true source of grace on our journey. That is why She leads us to the sacraments, for it is only through grace that we are perfected. Confession and communion then become the heart of our Christian life. Gospa has spoken about different types of prayer, especially the rosary. This prayer is truly put forward again after so many years of spirituality, for if we are called to imitate Christ, if we are called to become like Him, there is no better means than the rosary to pray to Him. The rosary is a mini-catechism of our faith. Every mystery of our faith is remembered anew and lived through the rosary: the Mystery of the Incarnation, the Mystery of the Passion, the Mystery of the

Resurrection. Thus, praying the rosary helps us to become like Mary. According to the Evangelist: "Mary quietly treasured these things in her heart and often thought about them" (Lk2,19, 51). I believe we are also called to remember these things in our hearts through the rosary. Thus prayer remains Christ-centered.

Our Lady told us we must seek two things: firstly, the Face of Our Lord. It is always dangerous to look at oneself, to consider what is good and just, for we do not realize that there is our "self" in this. That is why Gospa asks us to elevate our eyes and to look at Christ through prayer and so prayer must become Christ-centered. The second step, naturally becomes seeking God's will, for after meeting with God, we naturally arrive at the question:

"What do You want of me?"

During the rosary Gospa insists on silence, which is listening, not a moment of passivity but a total gift of oneself to the other through a greater capacity for listening. [...] In the human experience this is a very difficult matter, for we have the tendency to be the central figure. But I believe that the prayer of listening teaches us true adoration in order to understand who is the Author of life.

Penance always accompanies this prayer journey and thus becomes the prayer of the body. This term is undoubtedly not present in modern terminology. We are not used to doing penance for we believe that we are suffering enough as it is. However, to do penance, especially in moments of laziness, of spiritual sleep, is what shakes us up, what allows us to catch our breath and to persevere. That is why

Gospa insists so much on fasting, especially on bread and water. That is also full of significance. To live with material bread, in a sense, is but a waiting for the true bread we receive in the Eucharist. That is why the Eucharistic interpretation of this form of fasting, to me, is the most appropriate.

Questions of the witnesses — What interests me most are the experiences you had with the angel. How did you identify that presence as that of an angel? How did he speak to you? What was your reaction?

Jelena — *It is difficult to express it. I can only say that it is an inner recognition, an inner certitude that accompanies the gift. It is difficult not to recognize it.*

Q. — Did you have a particular sensation in a physical sense?

J. — *Really, no, not in the sense of an ecstasy or that type of experience, but I would say, rather of tranquillity, of peace, of joy, mostly feeling full of joy.*

Q. — You are in Rome. You know that in Italy there are many prayer groups. Many paths, and also the path of neo-catecumenism where we also speak of fasting and prayer. With whom are you grouping presently and what are you doing?

J. — *I must admit that I do not know the present ways of your country for the type of studies I am doing do not allow me time to lounge around (gi gironzolare). We formed a small informal group of friends among the students and we pray the rosary together. For me, in theory and in practice, the universality of the Church touches me and I do not see myself engaged on a well-defined path. Truly, I do not see myself involved in a spirituality that belongs to Medjugorje. It is our spirituality, Marian spirituality.*

Q. — We do not forget that Gospa guided Jelena on that path to holiness during many years.

J. — *Yes, but it is not a movement. Really, it is not a question of movement, and that is the beauty of Medjugorje, in order that all may participate.* [For Jelena, movement would seem to signify a closed group as political movements].

Q. — You spoke of silence. Speak to us about your experience with silence. These days, in Medjugorje, I believe I've experienced it. The silence of finding ourselves in His Presence and of feeling His physical Presence. Maybe because I began to pray here in a particular atmosphere. [...] But I truly felt a presence, a live image. Can you explain?

J. — *We cannot compare ourselves to anyone, because God calls us all singularly. I do not know exactly what you want me to say on silence or of standing before Gospa...in a passive manner. No, not in a passive manner.*

Q. — In the expectation of a message? Of something She will tell you in your heart?

J. — *Yes, but it is not programmed. It is a necessity, which comes to life. When we grow in our spiritual life, this necessity of receiving the Lord becomes spontaneous, for we are like children, we always need something. We ask: "Mommy, give me, give me this, give me this again." However, I believe there comes a moment of greater spiritual maturity when we are ready to receive. It is certainly a pathway and we must not become alarmed. It is a necessity, which comes.*

We abridged this improvised dialogue.

Q. — Gospa has used you as an instrument for the prayer group in Medjugorje for many years. In light of this experience, do you have any suggestions for our prayer groups?

J. — *I have never really elaborated a synthesis of what I have lived. I can only say that the prayer group seems to me an inevitable experience for spiritual growth. It is not possible to imagine a solitary journey with the Lord. God* calls us to a communion with others and so we are called to be in a prayer group. This can be with family, and the family should be the first prayer group where we are given the first spirituality. Then on a parish level, for it is in our immediate Church and in our parish where there should be different groups. I am speaking only of community needs, but the format depends on the spirituality you possess. The rosary is always useful, as well as spontaneous prayers, but the reading of the Bible is important, because our prayer must not be arbitrary, but must have a precise content, which is revealed to us. It is not like Oriental religions where our spirits can float (sempre vagare). We must remain faithful to the Gospel. Then we must have the opportunity of exchanging our experiences to encourage one another on our spiritual journey. This sharing is a communion in Christ, but also a true communion between us.

Q. — How can you discern whether it is Jesus or Mary speaking, and not a rebellious angel?

J. — *It is not difficult to discern. The presence of God always brings great peace and tranquillity, a sense of freedom and of fullness. The presence of the other brings about anguish and darkness.*

Q. — Do you still have visions of the heart?

J. — *They are not as frequent, but I still do have them.*

Q. — How did you choose to study in Vienna and then Rome?

J. — *I don't know. I certainly wanted to do God's will on every level. Spiritual life must not be separate from daily life. It was pleasing for me to transfer this spiritual experience into a concrete life, including research at an intellectual level, because intelligence is an integral part of our humanity. I should say: if you undertake a journey, seek what the Church has to say about it, the Magisterium, for we all need a guide. We are not self-sufficient and Christ wants it that way. From the very beginning, he always clearly indicated that He wanted a hierarchical Church and a Holy Father. It seemed good for me to include my experience in the experience of the whole Church [the history], for all these gifts are for the growth of the Church. Then, to be in Rome was a special grace because that is where the heart of the Church resides. Everything is linked.*

Q. — Have you ever considered getting married?

J. — *I have from time to time.*

Q. — There is a difficulty of dialogue in our group, maybe because it is too big?

J. – *Yes, that is true and the same is happening to our prayer group (in Medjugorje they number 60). For sharing, we split into smaller groups where we could more easily share our experiences.*

A priest. — Am I right in letting the groups fend for themselves *(da soli)*?

J. — *No, I don't think so. You are a priest, a guide is precious, and people need a guide even if everyone around us is screaming: "freedom, independence!" We need a guide and when one is missing, we become attached to strange things...unruly things. We need something to propel us forward, especially young people. It is a precious gift to have someone available to help shed a little light. This does not mean that a prayer group must do things your way. That would be another mistake. But in Medjugorje, Gospa has always asked for spiritual guides for groups.*

OPEN LETTER FROM THE *QUEEN OF PEACE COMMITEE*,

SIGNED BY BISHOPS FRANE FRANIC, PAOLO HNILICA AND 5 FRANCISCANS. (EXCERPTS) JULY 25, 1997

This letter expresses the deep affection which links us to the message of Medjugorje. Knowing that many others (bishops, priests, religious and laity) have gratefully witnessed on numerous occasions the spiritual fruit that has sprung from this message, we wished to share in writing a common witnessing, which is in itself a contribution to the work of Our Lady which spreads all over the world, but continues to be threatened.

No one can deny (even if there are some who attempt to do so) that the spiritual movement of the Queen of Peace is a living reality in the Church, born from a spirit of prayer and not of human initiative. [...] But how is it possible that the Franciscan parish of such a tiny village has become for the whole world a beacon, signaling a vast and effective call to prayer again. [...]

[...] It is by the grace of God that this oasis of peace has become a place of Marian devotion where we pray and are converted the most. [...]

The attitude of those who allow themselves to lay condemning judgements on Medjugorje cause a lot of suffering and leave too many faithful perplexed and disoriented. Once again last year, ambiguous allegations, at times edited in a distorted manner by a certain press, wanted to have us believe that an official condemnation of the apparitions had been handed down by the Church, or that serious doubts existed as to their true nature.

It is for this reason that in August 1996, the Holy Father's official speaker, Dr. Navarro Valls, had to intervene to confirm: "With regards to Medjugorje, nothing new was decided" [...] This providential communication from the Vatican reaffirmed that everyone could go on a private pilgrimage to Medjugorje, in other words that the laity can continue to organize their pilgrimages to that place of prayer.

The Queen of Peace did not come to Bosnia-Herzegovina to spread discord [...] in the Church, but to propose a message of peace and of reconciliation. A few years later the people were thrown into the hell of civil war... for her voice had cried as in the wilderness. She had come to warn [...] that, without true conversion of the heart, there could be no true peace. The peace that existed at the time (1981) was only apparent. [...] We did not understand. [...] the urgent necessity of returning to God for true peace. On June 26, 1981, Gospa appeared in tears before a huge Cross. On June 26, 1991, the first bombs fell on the airport of Ljubljana in Slovenia. [...] "Medjugorje is the continuation of Fatima," said the Holy Father John-Paul II to Bishop Hnilica, SJ in 1984. Many times the Pope has spoken favorably of Medjugorje with cardinals, bishops, priests and groups of faithful in private audiences. The Vicar of Christ, so attentive to the course of history, has never hesitated to show his love for the message of Medjugorje.

"Protect Medjugorje," he said to Fra Jozo Zovko, the Franciscan who paid for his fidelity to the apparitions of Medjugorje with imprisonment. He was the parish priest in 1981. Not only has Pope John-Paul II demonstrated his benevolence towards Medjugorje, but he has also expressed more than once, (including to the president of Croatia who recently attested to this), his desire to visit Medjugorje. [...] The Mother of God continues to encourage us to follow the Pope, the Vicar of Christ. [...] Medjugorje has become, as Fatima has, an international prayer center and a spiritual support for the universal Church [...]

One of the reasons for which the Queen of Peace came to the village of Medjugorje was to confirm the Pope's motto, *Totus tuus*, [All for You], to support him in the great task which the Lord has entrusted him with [...] to guide the Church into the next millenium. [...]

The pilgrims of Medjugorje have thus been given a great responsibility, that of bearing the fruit of the gift of prayer which Our Lady, Queen of Peace, has brought to Medjugorje: prayer of the heart and penance. [...]

We must not be surprised if we see Satan trying to destroy the supernatural fruit, which has ripened inside the spiritual movement of Medjugorje. In order to protect ourselves, we have to truly love, serve and imitate Our Queen and Mother of Peace by living Her messages which invite us to conversion through prayer, through fasting and total abandonment to the will of God to attain peace.

We must not be troubled by the lies being spread concerning Medjugorje. We must simply answer by the truth of our Christian life. [...] We know very well that voices are raised against Medjugorje. This is not the first time that disagreements have arisen against an event, even amongst bishops. Let us rely especially on the discernment of the supreme Pastor, Pope John-Paul II, who has never shown any doubt on the supernatural character of those events.

The Holy Father said, speaking to a medical Commission a few years ago: "The world is losing its sense of the supernatural. People rediscover it in Medjugorje, through prayer, fasting and the sacraments". [...]This commission had concluded that the phenomenon was unexplainable from a human point of view. It was the first time that scientific instruments had been used to examine visionaries in ecstasy during an apparition.

This message was edited on June 25th by three of the commission's secretaries, but was not published in English until July 7th, and in Croatian on July 21, 1997 in Slobodna Dalmacija. *Soon afterwards, the vicar general of Mostar, Dom Luka Pavlovic, expressed his criticism in the same newspaper, September 12, 1997, page 12. He particularly deplored the fact that the document referred to the Pope in a matter of controversy against the Bishop, and assures that there were few echoes (p.21).*

Signed by bishops Frane Franic and Hnilica; Father Tomislav Pervan, Herzegovina provincial; Ivan Landeka, pastor of Medjugorje; Slavko Barbaric; Jozo Zovko and Leonard Orec, the last five being Franciscans.

INTERVIEW WITH IVAN

February 1, 1997 in Medjugorje

Gebetsaktion — Ivan, you have been away from Medjugorje for some time. Where were you?

Ivan — *I spent 5 months in America where I participated in many prayer gatherings in many states and in many churches. I want to bring to everyone the messages, and everything that the Mother of God has been inviting us to for the last 15 years, so that they may understand, accept and bring it into reality. That is my mission.*

G. — What are people seeking?

I. — *People are thirsting for God. When they hear the messages from the Mother of God and what they are being invited to, they are satisfied by this spiritual nourishment, and renew their lives. They begin to pray, and once again peace and love have a place in their families.*

This spiritual food is quite necessary in our time. I would particularly like to draw attention to the Holy Mass, representing the center of our life, monthly confession, daily prayer, sacrifice and fasting. I would like to renew these words at every gathering. Over the last 15 years, the Mother of God has shown us the way which we must take.

We must choose it. She encourages us. How many times did she mention prayer in her messages!

However the message always renews itself, becoming a new guide. It is most important to understand it. As in the Gospel where Jesus rejoins his apostles and finds them asleep, the Mother of God would like to shake us up by her messages, which she has been entrusting to Marija for the last 25 months.

G. — What do you think of prayer?

I. — *Prayer is a continuous process. We cannot learn prayer in 20 years, nor in 50, not even 70. Our prayer will not be accomplished until our death. Prayer is a grace; it is a gift received. As far as I'm concerned, prayer is a meeting with God, a dialogue with Him. Each time people decide to pray, that moment must become a meeting with God, a communication creating a new relationship, a new confidence, a new opening of ourselves, a new repentance from sin. I would also say a new joy, a new love.*

That is what prayer means; but no one among us is perfect. We are all people who should strive to improve, to become more holy and above reproach. Prayer is a school in which we should practice every day. At the school of prayer there are no holidays, no weekends.

I pray every day as the Mother of God wishes: morning, noon and night. It is very important to persevere when we have chosen her direction, because we will always have time for the things we love. That is why it is so important for us to decide for God with all our heart.

G. — Ivan, you have said that the Mother of God asks us to pray three hours a day. Was that wish addressed to you, to prayer groups or to all people?

I. — *In 1984, before going to Holy Mass, the Mother of God came to me, asking me to tell the priests that she wished for all of us to pray for three hours every day.*

Through prayer, we assist Our Lady in the realization of her projects together with us — with the world — especially in the present times, for the world today imposes its lifestyle on us. People have turned to materialism and have given God second place. I believe that prayer, especially the rosary to which Our Lady invites us, is of the first importance. Prayer is a remedy, a holy medication for the world today.

G. — What subjects does the Mother of God speak to you about?

I. — *During my daily meetings with the Mother of God, we pray together for peace in the world, for youth, for families, for the conversion of sinners and for those for whom nobody prays. We know of the monthly messages, which She gives to Marija. Thus we know what Our Lady wishes, what is most important. We must take it into consideration and follow it. On the other days, Our Lady makes things clear for us visionaries. We have been in communion with Her for the last 15 years. We speak about a great many things, even about our private lives. Our Lady repeats to us what She announces on the 25th.*

G. — You have been in America with your family for some time. How long do you intend on remaining in Medjugorje?

Ivan with wife Maureen.

I. — *I'm only staying a short while, two weeks. On February 14th, I'm leaving for Australia, Hong Kong and Taiwan. I would like to transmit the messages of the Mother of God to the people in those countries as well. That is my goal.*

Just as Vicka and Father Slavko toured a part of Africa, I would like to travel to another continent to bring the joyful messages of the Queen of Peace. The message is truly joyful. At every meeting we feel joy and gratitude.

G. — How was the prayer group formed?

I. — *It was on July 4, 1982. My friends had suggested we go for a walk in the mountain. Spontaneously we started off and once we had arrived at the summit, we prayed for a long time.*

A few months later the Mother of God began to guide our group.

G. — What does the Mother of God say to the prayer group? What are the most important messages?

I. — *I believe that it is of the utmost importance that the whole family becomes a prayer group. The Mother of God repeats this constantly. When we pray as a family, problems don't exist. Today we must save our families and our young people. The Mother of God invites us to this and begs priests to inspire people to pray. Many other activities should be proposed outside the lessons of the catechism.*

The education of children must be a process in which we invest a lot of time and love. Education is the living Gospel. As children grow, we must tell them what is essential. We know to what point bad company, drugs and alcohol influence children. We must pray as a family! We must ask the question: how do the parents live, what harmony is there between the parents? To educate the children in truth it is important for parents to pray together in order to perceive through grace how to raise their children. The father must be the shepherd of the family who meets Jesus

Christ, who must find in wisdom the just pathway, who must explain good and evil, but with love so that the child might understand.

Sometimes the Mother of God asks for our prayers for her projects. She asks for unity, love, harmony and solidarity. We must give up the world through prayer. We must make it more secure and better, because it is a fact that the world cannot exist without God.

I say: "Nothing works without God! When we have decided for God, everything will flourish again. Goodness and peace will reign." This certainly gives us a perspective for a better world. God did not give us power in order to lead ourselves into anarchy. The purpose of power is a better world.

I would like to conclude by saying: let us follow the call of the Mother of God! She is not tired. She invites us endlessly. She is full of patience, of love and tenderness. Let us decide! By practicing her teachings, we will learn and we will see many things!

(Interview conducted by I.D.
Medjugorje #45, p. 16-20)

INTERVIEW WITH MONSIGNOR AUGUSTIN HARRIS, BISHOP EMERITUS OF MIDDLESBOROUGH

PUBLISHED IN MEDJUGORJE #43 (EXCERPTS)

Father Slavko. — What motivated you to come to Medjugorje?

Msgr. Harris. — *Curiosity. My friends came many times to Medjugorje, and this time I decided to come with them in private. They organized a pilgrimage to Medjugorje and they asked me if I wanted to be their spiritual director. Thus, last week I accompanied 103 pilgrims, and this week I am in charge of a group of 75 pilgrims.*

F.S. — What impressions did you get?

Msgr. Harris. — *I realized that we must tirelessly motivate the pilgrims to reflect on prayer and to allow the words of the rosary and of the Holy Mass to become a reality. I noticed something else. In Lourdes, for example, the grotto constitutes the center of that holy place. In Medjugorje, I have the impression that center is lacking. Here, we allow homes and hotels to be built around the*

Bishop Augustin Harris (left) with Fr. Slavko.

church. In a few years, there will be little room left for the pilgrims. I see a danger in this.

F.S. — What are your impressions when you look at the pilgrims?

Msgr. Harris. — *We pray here a lot, but we also pray in Lourdes or in my hometown. On the other hand, what becomes obvious in Medjugorje is the inner need for confession. Pilgrims here are ready to go deep within themselves and to do penance. In this way, I am convinced that many take a new and better route. However, priests must continually indicate to the pilgrims the fact that confession is not the end of a spiritual process of conversion, but the beginning. Pilgrims must leave this place with the firm resolution to continue to pray at home, in their families and in prayer groups. To lead them in this direction is the responsibility of every priest. It would be insufficient to teach people about Christ. We must teach them to pray more and pray more fervently to experience Christ in prayer.*

F.S. — It is a known fact that the local bishop adopts a position of rejection of Gospa's apparitions.

Msgr. Harris. — *I am not allowed to judge the bishop. My point of view is the following: we cannot say "NO" when someone comes here to pray, or for confession, and maybe change their whole life.*

F.S. — As a bishop, what do you advise people to do?

Msgr. Harris. — *Many people have certain fears when the time comes to give a verdict for or against Medjugorje. I personally believe that Medjugorje is an ideal place to unburden one's conscience. The pilgrims that I see here are the best proof. Does Gospa really appear here? I cannot say, but I have no reason to doubt the apparitions. I met a visionary who made a very positive impression on me. It is difficult to imagine that she has been lying for all these years.*

If people ask me whether they can go to Medjugorje, I can only answer: if you want to unburden your conscience and leave all your woes, then go!

Yesterday for the feast of the Exaltation of the Cross, I saw more than 50 Franciscan priests hearing confessions. It was an unforgettable sight! Today immediately after celebrating mass, a pilgrim approached me for confession. Could I say no? That is why I advise priests to serve the faithful, teach them to pray, be ready to hear confessions and everything will be positive.

CHRONOLOGY

1997
May

May	Sister Emmanuel in the USA and Mexico.
May 11	Presentation in Medjugorje of a monography of photos.
May 29	Commemoration of the three Italians killed on a humanitarian convoy during the war in Bosnia (3rd anniversary: see DN 14).
	Vicka in Zagreb for her mother's operation.

June

June 12-14	Slavko and Vicka, three days in Holland (*Eco* 134c; P 69-2).
June 24	March for peace.
June 25	16th anniversary of the first apparition.

July

July 1-6	First international retreat for priests with Father Slavko and Don Cosimo Cavaluzzo. The spiritual success of the retreat has encouraged organizers to repeat the experience each year from Jun 30-Jul 6th. 120 priests were present for this first international retreat.
July 4	Ivan celebrates his prayer group's 15th anniversary (E, July 15th).
July 18	Birth of Marco Maria Lunetti, Marija's third son, in Italy.
July 21-24	Week of formation for pilgrimage guides.

July

July 25   Feast of St. James, patron of Medjugorje parish.

October

Oct. 1   Marija in Medjugorje with her 3 children until after All-Saints day.

Oct. 2   Apparition to Mirjana at the Blue Cross at the foot of Podbrdo at 10:30. Prayer for unbelievers (E October 15th, *Eco* 136, 6a). The preceding was at her home.

Father Kraljevic, first animator and historian of Medjugorje, was appointed to the parish. He was the guardian of the convent in Siroki Brijeg. Grinko Koracic replaced him.

Oct.18-21   Sister Emmanuel in Quebec.

Oct. 22   Sister Emmanuel's conference on the contribution of Medjugorje to world peace, at the invitation of Washington congressmen.

Oct. 22   Pilgrimage of 1,200 French people.

Oct. 25   Until November 25th: *Eighth Hispanic Congress* in Medjugorje: 400 to 500 persons from 20 nations (*Eco* 137 5a).

November

Nov. 1   Father Jozo's trip to the USA. He visits Chicago and a dozen other parishes.

Vicka returns from a long journey in USA.

Nov. 3-10   Slavko in Germany (his journal is published in Medjugorje 47, p.14-15).

Nov. 9-15   Seventh meeting of the Centers of Peace, coming from all countries.

Nov. 25   First broadcast of *Radio Medjugorje*, directed by Fr. Miljenko (*Eco* 137, 5c).

Nov. 30   Jozo Zovko speaks at Reggio Emilia, in Italy, before 2,000 people.

December

Dec. 7   End of year retreat by Slavko at *Domus Pacis*.

Dec. 15   Seminar of fasting and prayer organized by Slavko at *Domus Pacis*, following a formula which continues since 1991 and is renewed several times yearly.

Dec. 29   Student retreat at *Domus Pacis*.

1998

January

Vicka in Italy.

Jan. 12-24   Slavko leaves for Poland with some of Sr. Elvira's young rehabilitated drug-addicts.

Jan. 18-22   Fr. Jozo preaches a retreat for priests in Medjugorje, which he will repeat in February for anglophones and many other times during the year.

Jan. 31   Sister Emmanuel leaves for Malaysia, Singapore and Australia to speak on the Heart of Mary, according to the message of Medjugorje.

February

Feb. 1	Bonifacio leaves for Poland.
Feb. 25-26	Slavko leaves for Germany with Vicka (E, March 1, 1998).

March

March 1	Conference with Ivan at the University of Steubenville (Ohio, USA).
	Monsignor Edwin O'Brien, Archbishop of the Armed Forces (USA), gives witness on Medjugorje (p. 87).
March 2	Mirjana has her monthly apparition at Los Gatos (California), with 50 persons.
March 5	Vicka leaves for Brazil and will return on the 16th.
March 8-12	Meeting of international leaders of Medjugorje at Neum.
March 17	Gospa asks Vicka to accept an interruption of apparitions until June 6th. The visionary accepts good-heartedly, but the sacrifice is great.
March 18	Apparition to Mirjana at 2 p.m. on basketball court of Sister Elvira's Cenacle: large crowd.

April

April 5-7	Sister Emmanuel's conferences in Bordeaux, Niort and Toulouse.
April 12	Easter — Ivan returns for the summer, but Marija, kept away by her three sons, could not come as in preceding years. She came at the end of the month.

May

May 24   Slavko in Palavobis with one of the visionaries to direct a day of fasting and prayer.

June

June 24   Walk for peace.

June 25   Celebration of 17th anniversary.

June 30   Beginning of second retreat for priests at Mary's school.

July

July 6   End of this retreat.

July 31   Beginning of Youth Festival in Medjugorje.

August

Aug. 6   End of Youth Festival on Krizevac at sunrise.

September

Sep. 11   Jakov Colo receives last secret and regular apparition from Our Lady while on speaking tour in Florida.

A VIDEO FILM AGAINST MEDJUGORJE

Monsignor Peric's action has mobilized and guided the adversaries with a new efficiency: a video film against Medjugorje, *Visions on Demand*, appears with a noisy propaganda, which lists the following themes:

Proof that Medjugorje is a fraud.

A video which unmasks the most notable false apparition and mystification of the century.

Shocking but true story of greed, lies and manipulation of religions, etc.

We find new protagonists among the collaborators: Maurice Alexander (42 years old), *Network 5*, Liverpool; his two associates Jeff Pickett and Michael Grymes, 22 years old and sponsor Phil Kronzer, mobilized old adversaries, the esteemed Father Hugh Thwait and Michael Jones, director of *Fidelity*, who rehashes his old arguments of which I presented the foolishness in DN 7, p. 42, p. 36-43. He underlines the argument under which Jozo Zovko and the Tomislav Vlasic would have introduced the *Charismatic Renewal* in that parish to enflame the hallucination. Jozo Zovko is spiritual, but is not involved in the Charismatic Renewal. Tomislav Vlasic, very much involved with the *Charismatic Renewal*, purposely avoided all interference of charismatic activities in order to dedicate himself to the spiritual awakening of the parish which remains one of the most admirable phenomenon of the 20th century. It would be self-degrading and degrading for the reader to attach anymore importance to this slander.

END OF DAILY APPARITIONS FOR JACOV COLO

Bravo!

On the 12th of September, feast of Our Lady's Holy Name, Jacov Colo (27 years old), received the 10th and final secret from Our Lady. She also told him she would not be appearing to him on a daily basis but rather once a year on Christmas day.

Jacov, the youngest of the Medjugorje visionaries (the only one under 30), and a father since September of 1996, was on a tour of the U.S. with Mirjana and Father Kraljevic. The event occured in Miami (Florida) in a private home.

During the evening of September 11, Our Lady asked Jacov to prepare himself through prayer. Our Lady was very sad as she revealed the 10th and final secret to Jacov. This is how Jacov related the message:

> *"On Friday September 11th during the regular apparition Our Lady told me to prepare myself specially by prayer for tomorrow's apparition because she will confide the 10th secret to me. On Saturday September 12th Our Lady came at 11:15 (local time). When she came she greeted me as always with 'Praised be Jesus'. While she was confiding the 10th secret to me she was sad.*
>
> *Then with a gentle smile she said to me: Dear child! I am your mother and I love you unconditionally. From today I will not be appearing to you every day, but only on Christmas, the birthday of my Son. Do not be sad, because as a mother I will always be with you and like every true mother I will never leave you. And you continue further to follow the way of my Son, the way of peace and love and try to persevere in the mission that I have*

confided to you. Be an example of that man
who has known God and God's love.

Let people always see in you an example of
how God acts on people and how God acts
through them. I bless you with my motherly
blessing and I thank you for having
responded to my call."

The apparition lasted 30 minutes. Jacov who usually tries to control his emotional nature, was absolutely overwhelmed. There is a deep sadness in him from the lack of daily contact with Our Heavenly Mother. He told Father Slavko that he wept bitterly during the apparition.

Jacov is thus the third visionary to have received all ten secrets, which also brings about the end of the daily apparitions. The first was Mirjana on Christmas day, 1982, followed by Ivanka on May 7th 1985.

The date of the yearly apparition differs for the three visionaries. For Mirjana it occurs on her birthday (March 18), for Ivanka it's the anniversary of the first apparition (June 25) and for Jacov it's Christmas day.

In 1985, everyone expected the other four visionaries to receive the tenth secret in a very short time followed by the rapid manifestation of those secrets. That was especially imagined with regards to the "Permanent Sign" which will be visible and permanent on the Hill of Apparitions. But 13 years have now gone by since Ivanka received the tenth secret. Three (daily) visionaries now remain: Vicka, Marija and Ivan.

What can we conclude from this?

1. One could ask if the end of Jacov's daily apparitions signifies something serious concerning the end of the apparitions themselves. One could be led to conclude that as Our Lady ceased appearing to Mirjana after 18 months, Ivanka after three years and Jacov after 13 years, the time is still quite far away as for the

other three visionaries, taking us almost to the year 2050 and beyond.

I do not believe this and it is more than probable that the frequency will be much quicker. The last three visionaries could even possibly receive the tenth secret simultaneously and the tenth secret revealed before the year 2000. Every hypothesis is possible. Our Lady has often left us with miscalculations as she is always mysterious and gratuitous. This is also a positive argument in favour of the authenticity of her apparitions.

2. What does this mean for Jacov? Two very important facts:

a) Since 1984, and especially during the last few years, many have been seriously questioning whether or not the visionaries were still seeing Our Lady. Were the apparitions being maintained mechanically through well-rehearsed mental controls and imagination? Is it possible that the ecstacies are being artificially perpetuated with charismatic well-groomed techniques?

I could not believe this for Ivan and Vicka with whom I have been very close for many years. The doubt could however be cast over to Jacov whose mysterious nature and private apparitions in his home could lead some to question their authenticity. The end of the apparitions for him not only destroys this hypothesis but also tends to confirm that Our Lady's apparitions were authentic. On September 12th, Gospa took leave of her visits as simply as they had begun.

b) Jacov has returned to ordinary faith, without signs or markings of a charismatic nature, such as for Bernadette [of Lourdes] on the 7th of April 1858, except for her final apparition on the 16th of July 1858. It is thus the end of the extraordinary for Jacov, a return to starless nights without the presence of a Comet of the first magnitude.

All our prayers are with Jacov on his return to an austere path to normal faith. This was asked also of Bernadette and almost every visionary with the exception of Estelle Faguette (Du Laus) and a few others who had apparitions up to the time they died.

Medjugorje leads us to faith and not to a creed of visions, signs and apparitions.

"Happy are those who have not seen yet believe." (John 20, 23)

Miami, Florida Sept. 12/98: Jakov during his last daily apparition. Wife Annalisa and daughter Arianna can be seen (son David is in his mother's arms).

ANNUAL APPARITION TO JAKOV ON DECEMBER 25, 1998

After the apparition which began at 11.50 a.m. and lasted 12 minutes, Jakov wrote:

"Our Lady came joyful. She greeted me, as always, with 'Praised be Jesus!' She spoke to me about the secrets and afterwards gave me this message:

'Dear children! Today, on the birthday of my Son, my heart is filled with immeasurable joy, love and peace. As your mother, I desire for each of you to feel that same joy, peace and love in the heart. That is why do not be afraid to open your heart and to completely surrender yourself to Jesus, because only in this way can He enter into your heart and fill it with love, peace and joy. I bless you with my motherly blessing.' "

Jakov prayed with his family. He prepared himself for the apparition with Confession and Holy Mass. After the apparition, he cried for a while.

ANNUAL APPARITON TO MIRJANA SOLDO ON MARCH 18, 1999

"Dear children! I want you to surrender your hearts to me so that I may take you on the way which leads to the light and to eternal life. I do not want your hearts to wander in today's darkness. I will help you. I will be with you on this way of discovery of the love and the mercy of God. As a mother, I ask you to permit me to do this. Thank you for having responded to my call."

The apparition lasted for 6 minutes from 10:14 to 10:20 am. Our Lady spoke about the secrets. She blessed everyone.

STATEMENT ON THE TESTS PERFORMED ON THE VISIONARIES

INSTITUTE FOR THE FIELD LIMITS OF SCIENCE (IGW) - INNSBRUCK;

CENTER FOR STUDY AND RESEARCH ON PSYCHOPHYSIOLOGY OF STATES OF CONSCIOUSNESS - MILANO;

EUROPEAN SCHOOL OF HYPNOTIC PSYCHOTHERAPY AMISI OF MILAN;

PARAPSYCHOLOGY CENTER OF BOLOGNA.

At the request of the Parish Office of Medjugorje psychophysiological and psychodiagnostic research was carried out on the subjects who since 1981 are known as the visionaries' group of Medjugorje. The research was carried out in four sessions:

The first research was carried out on April 22-23, 1998 at the Casa Incontri Cristiani [House of Christian Encounters] in Capiago Intimiano (Como), which is operated by the Dehonian Fathers. On this occasion the examined were: Ivan Dragicevic, Marija Pavlovic Lunetti, and Vicka Ivankovic.

The second research was carried out from on July 23-24, 1998 in Medjugorje.

Examined were Mirjana Soldo-Dragicevic, Vicka Ivankovic and Ivanka Elez-Ivankovic.

The third research, only psychodiagnostic, was conducted by psychologist Lori Bradvica on Jakov Colo with the collaboration of Fr. Ivan Landeka.

The fourth psycho-physiological registration was conducted Dec. 11, 1998 in the same House of Christian Encounters in Capiago Intimiano (Como) with Marija Pavlovic.

The incompleteness of the psycho-physiological investigation was caused by the partial cooperation of some subjects who did not undergo what the working group had expected, due either to their family or social obligations or to their personal reluctance, even though Fr. Slavko Barbaric and Fr. Ivan Landeka encouraged them to do it, without any influences on the programs of the working group called "Medjugorje 3", because, apart from individual medical or psychological investigation, prior to this research two groups had operated: the first a group of French doctors in 1984, and the second a group of Italian doctors in 1985. In addition three European psychiatrists in 1986 carried out only psychiatro-diagnostic investigations.

The following collaborated in the "Medjugorje 3" work group:

• Fr. Andreas Resch, theologian and psychologist from Institute for the Field Limits of Science (IGW) — Innsbruck; General coordinator;

• Dr. Giorgio Gagliardi, medical psychophysiologist from the Center for Study and Research on Psychophysiology of States of Consciousness — Milano; member of board of European School of Hypnotic Psychotherapy AMISI, Milan and of the Parapsychology Center of Bologna;

• Dr. Marco Margnelli, medical psychophysiologist and neurophysiologist from the Center for Study and Research on States of Consciousness — Milano, member of the professors' board of the European School AMISI, Milan;

• Dr. Mario Cigada, psychotherapist and oculist, Milano, member of the professorial board of the European School AMISI, Milano;

• Dr. Luigi Ravagnati, neurologist; assistant for neurosurgery at the University of Milan, member of the professors' board of the European School of Hypnotic Psychotherapy AMISI, Milan;

- Dr. Marianna Bolko, psychiatrist and psychoanalyst, instructor for specialization in psychotherapy at the University of Bologna;

- Dr. Virginio Nava, psychiatrist; head doctor at Como Psychiatric Hospital;

- Dr. Rosanna Constantini, psychologist, instructor at Auxilium University, Rome;

- Dr. Fabio Alberghina, medical internist;

- Dr. Giovanni Li Rosi, gynecologist at Varese Hospital and specialist for hypnotic psychotherapy, AMISI, Milan;

- Dr. Gaetano Perriconi, internist at FBF Hospital in Erbi/Como;

- Prof. Massimo Pagani, medical internist, professor of internal medicine at the University of Milan;

- Dr. Gabriella Raffaelli, scientific secretary;

- Fiorella Gagliardi, secretary, community assistant.

The following tests were used on the subjects to investigate their actual psychophysical and psychological situation:

- complete case history,

- medical case history,

- MMPI, EPI, MHQ; Tree test, Person test, Raven Matrixes, Rorschach Test, Hand test, Valsecchi truth and lie detection test;

- neurological visit,

- computerized polygraph (skin electrical activity; peripheral cardiac capillary and heartbeat activities; skeletal and diaphragmatic pneumography) during the apparitional experience, during mediated hypnotic recall of the same apparitional experience.

- Holter's arterial pressure dynamic registration.

- Holter's electro-cardiographic/respiratory dynamic registration.
- pupillary reflexes (photomotor) and winking reflex
- video takes
- photographs

For all the tests performed the visionaries made their decision with full freedom, readiness and collaboration. The results from these psychological-diagnostic investigations show that:

During the period since age 17, from the beginning of their apparitional experiences, the subjects do not exhibit any kind of pathological symptoms like trance interference, disassociative interference and loss of reality interference.

All subjects investigated, however, exhibited symptoms that are related to justified stress that occurs through very high levels of exogenous and endogenous stimulation as a consequence of every day life.

From their personal testimonies it follows that the initial and subsequent altered state of consciousness occurs due to their unusual experiences which they themselves recognize and define and still continuously recognize as a vision/apparition of Our Lady.

The psycho-physical investigation was carried out on four states of consciousness:

- waking state;
- altered state of consciousness (hypnosis with investigation of the state of ecstasy);
- state of visualization of mental images;
- altered state of consciousness(defined as the ecstasy of apparition).

The aim was to investigate whether the ecstatic state of apparition, already registered in 1985 by the

Italian doctors working group, still continues to be present or has undergone changes. In addition it was desired to investigate potential coincidence/divergence with other states of consciousness such as guided visualization or hypnosis.

Results of the investigation carried out demonstrate that the ecstatic phenomenology can be compared to the one from 1985 with somewhat less intensity.

The hypnotically induced state of ecstasy did not cause the phenomenology of spontaneous experiences and therefore it can be deduced that the ecstatic states of spontaneous apparitions were not states of hypnotic trance.

Capiago Intimiano, December 12, 1998

(Undersigned) Fr. Andreas Resch, Dr. Giorgio Gagliardi, Dr. Marco Margnelli, Dr. Marianna Bolko, Dr. Gabriella Raffaelli.

Footnotes

Chapter 3

1. I say: "Bishop Peric" for more clarity, as he is the "master of ceremonies" and assumes the accusations in the letters he sends me, stamped with his official seal. I state precisely that the note is not signed by him but rather by those responsible in the diocese of Mostar under cover of the bishop.

2. Even if these reports are the basis for the decisions taken in Rome and enacted through the authority of the Franciscan Order. The Order was mobilised through obedience for the destruction of one of the most ancient, beautiful, and fervent province, rich in martyrs and confessors of the faith.

Chapter 5

1. Terry holds a fond memory of the feast of the Visitation, May 31, 1995. That day, Marija was at his home in Birmingham. After the apparition, he asked Marija to recite the Magnificat on this day when Our Lady pronounced it. After the apparition, he received the following message:

Dear children, I desire that through your lives, you become witnesses, that you become my extended hands, my instruments. Win over as many hearts as you can to My Heart and lead them to God on the road to salvation.

2. A complete relaxation: muscular, psychological, and spiritual

3. Her health returned with her normal speech, to everyone's surprise.

Chapter 9

1. These conclusions were those of the commission at the bishop's request, but not in the Bishop's name.

2. Same observation: the commission has no judicial authority.

3. It was at the Bishop's request that the Episcopal Conference published this statement with the concern that it was to be understood as a pure and simple prohibition of pilgrimages. Monsignor Franic, as a good canonist, explained that according to Church Law, only official pilgrimages were premature; private pilgrimages, even organized, were in no way prohibited.

4. I responded to this unilateral and slanderous article in DN 2.

5. I've always agreed with this point with which I dealt in my "Messages and Pedagogy of Our Lady in Medjugorje" (p. 319-337). Here again we must unfortunately recall the non-said: the chaplains had put forth a measure which seemed abusive to the Church's Supreme Court. Judgement was postponed for eight years by a high-level administrative authority. When the case was allowed to continue, the decision was declared contrary to Church law (DN 13, 349). The scandal caused by this miscarriage of justice brought about the loss of a vocation for one of the two priests who left the habit after being relieved of his three vows, of which one was chastity.

6. This text was the result of the persevering action (attested by paragraphs 3, 4, 5, 8), to have the apparent prohibition of pilgrimages published by the Roman press. That document avoided the distinction between official and private pilgrimages, which remain perfectly open to Christian freedom. We can see how often this ambiguous dissuasion was promoted, each time producting a halt or decrease in the pilgrimages organized by the laity.

7. This relation keeps to the negative, but omits signaling that the negative judgement (The supernatural has not been established) was refused by Cardinal Ratzinger who asked for the dissolution of the Commission and transferred the judgement to the Episcopal Conference of Yugoslavia (April 1986).

8. See note 6.

9. This quote demonstrates the controversial and aggressive tone of Bishop Zanic's confirmation sermon. The tirade against Medjugorje was a black mark on the sacrament of confirmation ceremony administered by the Bishop. I have included the translation of this homily with footnotes that will enlighten and complete the Bishop's point of view.

10. The Bishop's third declaration was published in DN 9, p. 142-169, with 35 footnotes that complete and explain this unilateral document's affirmations.

11. Declaration edited p. 24. Here again we omit what was said p. 38-40.

12. "Official," he justly clarifies. See p. 179 and note (3).

13. Monsignor Peric quite rightly notes that the opposition of the diocese of Mostar to Medjugorje stems from the unfortunate interferences which have arisen between the apparitions and the Herzegovina conflict. But the sanctions that Vicka had regretably declared to be "hasty," have been declared contrary to Church law by the Church's Supreme Court (DN13, p. 47-49 and below).

14. The text is censored. The bishops have said: considering the incomplete state of the Commission's studies: "On the basis of the investigations that have so far been established, we cannot affirm that we are dealing with genuine apparitions or supernatural revelations." The Episcopal conference thus confirms the Commission's ignorance, still unable to judge, but promises to continue it's studies. To state that this declaration excludes the supernatural is to contradict its own text and the interpretation authorized by Cardinal Kuharic, President of the Episcopal Conference (As established on pages 41-44).

15. Can we say that the fruit does not prove anything? That would entail forgetting the only principle of discernment, fundamentally given by Christ: "We recognize the tree by its fruit." It is regrettable that the fruit of Medjugorje was never seriously examined. It is exceptional and in many ways, incomparable. The principal aim of my Latest News has been to manifest this fruit, ignored or unknown by the

Commission, as indicated by this paragraph, tributary of this deficient investigation. If Bishop Peric had spent one or two afternoons hearing confession in Medjugorje, as all confessors, he would be convinced.

16. It is true that the messages of Medjugorje are repetitive and common: common because they do nothing but repeat the Gospels and its key points — faith, prayer, conversion, penance, fasting, reading and meditation of Scripture. They prophetically actualize and lead hundreds of thousands of faithful to practice the key points of the Gospel. That is in itself non-negligible fruit.

17. I've noted here the contradictions or lies with which the visionaries were trapped. Vicka would have said on June 30, 1981 that the apparitions would end in 3 days. During these troubled times, under the threat of the police, she meant the end of apparitions on the hill, an error of perspective, as can occur, even in the Bible.

18. On this point, as on the others, the text remains apart from the reality and minimizes it. To say that the six visionaries "remain normal as are all other normal faithful" is true in one sense. But among the normal faithful of our times, how many are regular practitioners, as are the visionaries or had long and serious engagements before deciding on a life's vocation? How many give so much time to daily prayer and such concern for Christian education in their family? At a time when faith is disappearing in so many Christian families, their fidelity, in spite of the difficulty of their situation as visionaries, is also a good argument; a favorable convergence for the apparitions.

19. Here again the document reduces and minimizes the phenomenon. We manifested its amplitude and perseverance without equal in chapter 5 of every volume of Latest News; see p. 100-104.

20. In an interview with Monsignor Franic, the publication *Gebetsaktion* questioned the fact that Monsignor Franic's episcopal town, very exposed, suffered no loss while the Bishop of Mostar's residence suffered terrible destruction

which did not spare the cathedral. I realize that this is not an argument; neither is the fact that Medjugorje was not touched although targeted, while the village of Citluk was severely bombarded. Can one see Providence in this? It is for each one to judge. This point has neither the evidence nor the value of the precedents.

21. The visionaries' comments on the end of the apparitions were ambiguous. June 30th marked the end of the apparitions on the hill, which was at the time a preoccupation for all, including the police. Did the visionaries intend to say more? I wouldn't think so.

The Bishop then suggests that the visionaries' ecstasy would be a managed artificial phenomenon. He refrains from saying, as others have, that the apparitions were authentic in the beginning and later prolonged out of habit, or as for him, by calculation. This doubt had never been emitted so radically. That a charism could be prolonged artificially (healing charism for instance) is a fact and a problem which should be closely examined. That is why I've always regretted the lack of co-operation of the visionaries and some of their advisors, which prevents them from continuing with the medical tests. It is not too late.

22. The pilgrims have founded their faith in God, not on the apparitions, which have awakened their sleeping faith. They attend daily mass in a Catholic Church and go to confession. Why caricaturize and slander their faith which should normally be respected and stimulated?

Nothing can be said on this diplomatic paragraph. At the beginning of the apparitions (when he believed in them), Bishop Zanic defended the visionaries against the civil authorities. Monsignor Peric warns the civil authorities against holding a biased belief.

23. By celebrating a pilgrimage Mass, in the name of the Episcopal Conference of Yugoslavia, the bishops, including future Cardinal Puljic and Monsignor Zanic, assumed the usual cult in Medjugorje without necessarily recognizing the

apparitions, as is done in many other sanctuaries where the cult is admitted without official recognition.

It is the Bishop's right to remind us that there can be preaching on the Blessed Virgin and on the messages of the Gospel, but not on the alleged apparitions.

The Bishop is obeyed in his demand that no official pilgrimage be organized (although the official celebration of the pilgrims' Mass by other bishops might lead to another conclusion.) Private pilgrimages accompanied by a priest remain open to Christian faith. We are reminded of this by Doctor Navarro-Valls, who speaks for the Holy See.

Moreover, as in Lourdes or in Fatima before the long awaited verdict, the faithful are free to personally believe in the apparitions with due respect to the future judgement of the Church. As to the Church's official declarations, they have no dogmatic authority as to the discernment of the apparitions' authenticity. In such matters, the Christian tradition and the norms of the Church give the faithful a freedom of opinion, as long as they observe the good order and authority of the Church along common guidelines.

24. We can only agree on this final conclusion which illustrates so well the Medjugorje pilgrimage.

25. Here again, the bishop gives the diocesan position, which does not involve an episcopal authority. It is a motivated opinion, yet personal and provisional. In matters of discernment, nuances are subtle since the official recognition of an apparition never constitutes dogma, nor an obligation to believe, even in the case of Lourdes or Fatima.

26. Much could be said about this crushing majority, if not crushed, at least solicited by the bishop's negative and public declarations. The negative vote was more than limited as the experts, having not acquired the certitude of the authenticity, answered negatively to the question but without excluding the supernatural being under investigation (see p. 44-46).

27. Here again, Dr. Novarro-Valls' declaration was not mentioned. Speaking for the Holy-See, he stated that private pilgrimages remain open to individual Christian freedom

and may be accompanied by a priest. Omissions disfigure the truth.

28. Although the positive aspects of Medjugorje are conveniently omitted in this letter, the negative is endlessly expounded. We cannot see what would preclude the visionaries from witnessing, an inherent right for all Christians with prudence and the necessary nuances. We would certainly like to see this prudence, asked of believers and sympathisers be practised by the unbelievers and the attackers.

29. Bishop Peric's opinion is not that of the Yugoslav bishops dated April 10th, 1991. It contradicts the position of Bishop Kuharic, President of that conference.

30. This nuance does honor to the bishop's prudence. He does not confuse his opinion with the authorised judgement as does the local bishop, successor of the apostles.

BIOGRAPHY OF THE AUTHOR

Since this is to be the last volume of Latest News *on* Medjugorje *by Fr. Laurentin, the publisher deems it appropriate to include the following biography of this most renowned theologian.*

René Laurentin was born in Tours, October 19, 1917, son of Maurice Laurentin, architect, and Mary Jactel (maiden name). He completed his secondary (high school) studies at St. Mary of Cholet Institute, entered the Seminary of Carmes at the Catholic Institute of Paris in October 1934, where he obtained his diplomas of Master of Thomistic Philosophy at the same time as his "Licence ès-Lettres Philosophie" at the Sorbonne (1938).

At the end of his first year of Theology (1937-1938) he served in the military as an Infantry Officer during the World War. He was decorated with the Military Cross, two citations and the Legion of Honor. He was taken prisoner in Belgium (May 1940), he spent five years in Germany, taught Hebrew at the University of Oflag, pursued his studies at the Seminary and started Mariology under the direction of Father Génévois O.P.

Condemned by a German war council in October 1944, for "Militär Widersetzung" (obstruction of military rules) he terminated his captivity in 1945 in the Fortress of Königstein which was also the camp for 60 French generals and where General Giraud escaped.

He received his diploma in Theology in July 1946, and was ordained to the priesthood December 8 by His Excellency Monsignor Blanchet, Rector of the Catholic Institute. He prepared his three theses (ès-Lettres and Theology) on the Virgin Mary, while traveling through the principal countries of Europe in search of documentation: From London to Seville, from Dreux to Paris, Innsbruck and Klagenfurt, from Louvain to Rome where he spent the winter of 1946-47.

He received his Doctor of ès-Lettres from the Sorbonne University, with very honorable mention on June 7, 1952, for two theses, one historical and the other icono-graphical on the sacerdotal problem of the Virgin. The Catholic Institute of Paris conferred on him the Diploma of Doctor of Theology "Cum Singulari Prorsus Laude" on February 9, 1953.

He was appointed professor of Theology at the Catholic University of Angers in October 1955, Vice President of the French Society of Marian studies in 1962, consultant to the preparatory commissions of Vatican II in 1960, then expert of council in 1962 to 1965. He became Columnist of the Council of Figaro from the spring of 1963. His second article (an editorial like the first) predicted the election of Paul VI.

L'Abbé Laurentin who was trained in classical theology was not inclined toward apparitions. "I did not search them out, they came and looked for me" he said. In 1953, Monsignor Théas asked him for "A Theology of Lourdes." The work required more than 30 volumes. It silences at once the persistent polemics of free thinking and renews the pastoral of Lourdes. This success determined the request for similar studies on Pontmain, the miraculous medal, and Fatima where he could only accept an advisory post. From 1983, in spite of himself, he became a specialist in current apparitions which multiply across the world.

In 1981 Rome authorized the reopening of the dossier of Yvonne-Aimée of Malestroit on whom a decree by the Holy Office had forbidden publication. He methodically pursued the rehabilitation (Eight published volumes).

He participated in numerous radio and television broadcasts in France, Germany, Argentina, Canada, Italy, Poland, Switzerland, the USSR (formerly), the USA and Venezuela.

He leads the front with university teaching and activity as a professional journalist (Card 37043). It is his open window on the world (more than 2,000 articles of which almost 1,000 in number are in the Figaro and several hundreds in 10 years in the Christian Magazine).

Persuaded that the life of the local churches, premises of living Tradition, is an indispensable source of Theology, he methodically visited the churches of 40 countries from East to West. He had begun a series of works through the publishing house, Editions du Seuil, on Latin America (before and after Medellin), on Israel, and on Asia (Flashes on the Extreme Orient), China and the USSR after Perestroika. He published several articles in Concilium, theological articles where he wrote an editorial and two articles with main emphasis on the church in Africa and on the situation of the youth.

Aware that theology demands a liturgical life and profound prayer, he practices a pastoral ministry in a contemplative convent in the suburbs of Paris.

AN HOMAGE VOLUME REVEALS
THE HIDDEN WORK OF L'ABBÉ LAURENTIN

A committee of sponsors, presided by His Eminence Cardinal Poupard, gathered together several cardinals and Academic experts to publish an homage volume in his honor (700 pages with Desclée).

On November 22, 1989, he was received by the Pontifical Theological Academy of Rome (he already belongs to two Mariological Academies in the same city).

THE RANGE OF RESEARCH

Appparently diverse and incongruous, his work is one sole look at God working in the life of men, which details a range of several aspects.

• the Word of God: the source, where we find the scientific work of biblical exegesis;

- the Virgin Mary, his best witness and the others: St. Louis Marie Grignion of Montfort, St. Catherine Labouré, St. Bernadette, Theresa, Yvonne-Aimée of Malestroit: the hidden life, the prayer (Ave Maria, at DDB, the Prayer at Desclée);

- but also the apparitions and charisms: the bizarre stigmata and bilocations in multi-disciplinary collaboration especially with the doctors. God has not finished surprising us, if we do not close our eyes, as the weight of our culture and our current philosophy invites us to do.

How can the Church and the world, suffering from illness, understand each other at last. (Theme of his book: The Church who comes, Desclée). It is there l'Abbé Laurentin makes explicit the ambiguous situation of the post Council Church and her future on the threshold of the post-Marxist era.

LITERARY AND THEOLOGICAL PRIZES RECEIVED BY RENÉ LAURENTIN

1983: Broquette Gonin Prize for: The Gospels of Childhood (Scientific work of exegesis)

Foreign Prizes

1964: Marian Award of the University of Dayton (Ohio, USA) for his work on the Virgin.

1974: Wlodzimieerze Pietrzak Prize (Warsaw) Awarded to a foreign writer for his overall work.

1984: Ecumenical Prize Sapienza (Italy)

1987: Magnificat Prize for his theological work awarded by the President of the Philippines, Cory Aquino, in the presence of Cardinal Sin, at the Presidential Palace, Manila.

1988: The Golden Pen of the Franco-Yugoslavian Friends

1996: Prize of Catholic Culture at Bassano di Grappa (Italy)

PUBLICATIONS

Too numerous to document here; hundreds of books, many hundreds of articles in diverse academic journals, reviews, and periodicals.

MESSAGE OF THE CARDINAL ARCHBISHOP OF LYON

At the Academic Session of Angers (November 24, 1989).

It gives me particular pleasure to associate myself, if not in person, to my regret, but at least by these few lines with the so well deserved homage solemnly rendered today to Monsieur l'Abbé René Laurentin. With what wonder, for many years, have I not read and reread, pen in hand, his short treatise on the Virgin Mary, with the essential studies on the two first chapters of St. Luke, fruits of an erudition so methodical, that nothing can escape the perspicacity of the healthy critic. Here, without doubt, we have the first quality of Father Laurentin: rigorous treatment, the passion of exhaustive investigation. We find it once more in the work — and what a work — of research on the apparitions of Our Lady at Lourdes. Here, the mingled talent of the historian and the authentic theologian combine in order to permit us to relive not only the unfolding events, but, thanks to a spiritual intuition, without contradiction to the seriousness of the method, to touch ultimately even the soul of Bernadette, to see, on occasion, those of the privileged witnesses. We may also advance, thanks only to him, Marianology, and also in Marian piety, linked to the sanctuary of Lourdes. We are in great debt to the labor of Father Laurentin.

Furthermore, who among us has not appreciated the exactitude of his chronicles of the Council of Vatican II. The finesse of his journalistic analysis and competence has permitted so many of the faithful to acquire the sense of the Church, while trudging day after day through the toils of the Fathers.

Others, more competent than I, will devote themselves to underline the numerous aspects of his works, with scholarly communications. I, on my part, wanted to underline the fact that he maintains the happy conjunction of scientific rigor, spiritual contemplation, and the zeal of a pastor. In presenting my heartfelt congratulations to dear Father Laurentin, I hope that with God's help he may continue with many more years, bringing his irreplaceable contribution and multiple service to the Church.

✠ Albert Cardinal Decourtray

Lyon, December 4, 1989